KINGDOM LIVING

Growing Steadfast in the Faith

A Study of Romans

Jack W. Hayford
with
William D. Watkins

THOMAS NELSON PUBLISHERS
Nashville

CONTENTS

About the General Editor/About the Writer 4

The Gift That Keeps on Giving 5

Lesson 1:   Introducing Romans 10

Lesson 2:   God's Great News (1:1–17) 25

Lesson 3:   No Excuses (1:18—2:16) 35

Lesson 4:   No Exceptions (2:17—3:20) 46

Lesson 5:   Getting Right with God (3:21—4:25) 51

Lesson 6:   When Death Brings Life (5:1–21) 64

Lesson 7:   Free at Last! (6:1—7:25) 79

Lesson 8:   Heirs of Glory (8:1–39) 93

Lesson 9:   Promises That Never Fail (9:1—11:36) 105

Lesson 10:   Transformed Sacrifices (12:1–21) 118

Lesson 11:   Citizenship for Pilgrims (13:1–14) 129

Lesson 12:   Liberating Love (14:1—15:13) 136

Lesson 13:   On the Road Again (15:14–33) 142

Lesson 14:   Greeting the Family of God (16:1–27) 151

Kingdom Living: Growing Steadfast in the Faith (A Study of Romans) is one of a series of study guides that focus exciting, discovery-geared coverage of Bible book and power themes—all prompting toward dynamic, Holy Spirit-filled living.

About the General Editor

JACK W. HAYFORD, noted pastor, teacher, writer, and composer, is the General Editor of the complete series, working with the publisher in the conceiving and developing of each of the books.

Dr. Hayford is Senior Pastor of The Church On The Way, the First Foursquare Church of Van Nuys, California. He and his wife, Anna, have four married children, all of whom are active in either pastoral ministry or vital church life. As General Editor of the *Spirit-Filled Life Bible,* Pastor Hayford led a four-year project, which has resulted in the availability of one of today's most practical and popular study Bibles. He is author of more than twenty books, including *A Passion for Fullness, The Beauty of Spiritual Language, Rebuilding the Real You,* and *Prayer Is Invading the Impossible.* His musical compositions number over four hundred songs, including the widely sung "Majesty."

About the Writer

WILLIAM D. WATKINS has been integrally involved in Christian ministry since 1975 as teacher, writer, and speaker. Formerly with Insight for Living and Thomas Nelson Publishers, he is currently Senior Acquisitions Editor with Moody Press and president of his own literary company, William Pens. He coauthored *Worlds Apart: A Handbook on World Views,* published by Baker Book House; at Insight for Living, he coauthored twenty-one study guides with Chuck Swindoll.

Bill has a B.A. in Philosophy from California State University at Fresno and a Th.M. in Systematic Theology from Dallas Theological Seminary. He and his wife, Pamela, have five children, ages 11–19. They reside in Smyrna, Tennessee.

Of this contributor, the General Editor has remarked: "Bill Watkins manifests such an evenhandedness in his opening of the Scriptures, it is satisfying to be assisted by his work in this project. His longtime experience *in* the Word, along with his obvious love *for* God's Word, is a benefit to us all."

THE GIFT
THAT KEEPS ON GIVING

Who doesn't like presents? Whether they come wrapped in colorful paper and beautiful bows, or brown paper bags closed and tied at the top with old shoestring. Kids and adults of all ages love getting and opening presents.

But even this moment of surprise and pleasure can be marked by dread and fear. All it takes is for these words to appear: "Assembly Required. Instructions Enclosed." How we hate these words! They taunt us, tease us, beckon us to try to challenge them, all the while knowing that they have the upper hand. If we don't understand the instructions, or if we ignore them and try to put the gift together ourselves, more than likely, we'll only assemble frustration and anger. What we felt about our great gift—all the joy, anticipation, and wonder—will vanish. And they will never return, at least not to that pristine state they had before we realized that *we* had to assemble our present with instructions *no consumer* will ever understand.

One of the most precious gifts God has given us is His Word, the Bible. Wrapped in the glory and sacrifice of His Son and delivered by the power and ministry of His Spirit, it is a treasured gift—one the family of God has preserved and protected for centuries as a family heirloom. It promises that it is the gift that keeps on giving, because the Giver it reveals is inexhaustible in His love and grace.

Tragically, though, fewer and fewer people, even those who number themselves among God's everlasting family, are opening this gift and seeking to understand what it's all about and how to use it. They often feel intimidated by it. It requires some assembly, and its instructions are hard to comprehend sometimes. How does the Bible fit together anyway? What does Genesis have to do with Revelation? Who are Abraham and Moses, and what is their relationship to Jesus and Paul? And what about the works of the Law and the works of faith? What are they all about, and how do they fit together, if at all?

And what does this ancient Book have to say to us who are looking toward the twenty-first century? Will taking the time and energy to understand its instructions and to fit it all together really help you and me? Will it help us better understand who we are, what the future holds, how we can better live here and now? Will it really help us in our personal relationships, in our marriages and families, in our jobs? Can it give us more than just advice on how to handle crises? the death of a loved one? the financial fallout of losing a job? catastrophic illness? betrayal by a friend? the seduction of our values? the abuses of the heart and soul? Will it allay our fears and calm our restlessness and heal our wounds? Can it really get us in touch with the same power that gave birth to the universe? that parted the Red Sea? that raised Jesus from the stranglehold of the grave? Can we really find unconditional love, total forgiveness, and genuine healing in its pages?

Yes. Yes. Without a shred of doubt.

The *Spirit-Filled Life Bible Discovery Guide* series is designed to help you unwrap, assemble, and enjoy all God has for you in the pages of Scripture. It will focus your time and energy on the books of the Bible, the people and places they describe, and the themes and life applications that flow thick from its pages like honey oozing from a beehive.

So you can get the most out of God's Word, this series has a number of helpful features. Each study guide has no more than fourteen lessons, each arranged so you can plumb the depths or skim the surface, depending on your needs and interests.

The study guides also contain six major lesson features, each marked by a symbol and heading for easy identification.

 WORD WEALTH

The WORD WEALTH feature provides important definitions of key terms.

BEHIND THE SCENES

BEHIND THE SCENES supplies information about cultural beliefs and practices, doctrinal disputes, business trades, and the like that illuminate Bible passages and teachings.

 AT A GLANCE

The AT A GLANCE feature uses maps and charts to identify places and simplify themes or positions.

 BIBLE EXTRA

Because this study guide focuses on a book of the Bible, you will find a BIBLE EXTRA feature that guides you into Bible dictionaries, Bible encyclopedias, and other resources that will enable you to glean more from the Bible's wealth if you want something extra.

 PROBING THE DEPTHS

Another feature, PROBING THE DEPTHS, will explain controversial issues raised by particular lessons and cite Bible passages and other sources to which you can turn to help you come to your own conclusions.

 FAITH ALIVE

Finally, each lesson contains a FAITH ALIVE feature. Here the focus is, So what? Given what the Bible says, what does it mean for my life? How can it impact my day-to-day needs, hurts, relationships, concerns, and whatever else is important to me? FAITH ALIVE will help you see and apply the practical relevance of God's literary gift.

As you'll see, these guides supply space for you to answer the study and life-application questions and exercises. You may, however, want to record all your answers, or just the overflow from your study or application, in a separate notebook or journal. This would be especially helpful if you think you'll dig into the BIBLE EXTRA features. Because the exercises in this feature are optional and they can be expanded as far as you want to take them, we have not allowed writing space for them in this study guide. So you may want to have a notebook or journal handy for recording your discoveries while working through to this feature's riches.

The Bible study method used in this series revolves around four basic steps: observation, interpretation, correlation, and application. Observation answers the question, What does the text say? Interpretation deals with, What does the text mean?—not with what it means to you or me, but what it meant to its original readers. Correlation asks, What light do other Scripture passages shed on this text? And application, the goal of Bible study, poses the question, How should my life change in response to the Holy Spirit's teaching of this text?

If you have used a Bible much before, you know that it comes in a variety of translations and paraphrases. Although you can use any of them with profit as you work through the *Spirit-Filled Life Bible Discovery Guide* series, when Bible passages or words are cited, you will find they are from the New King James Version of the Bible. Using this translation with this series will make your study easier, but it's certainly not necessary.

The only resources you need to complete and apply these study guides are a heart and mind open to the Holy Spirit, a prayerful attitude, and a pencil and a Bible. Of course, you may draw upon other sources, such as commentaries, dictionaries, encyclopedias, atlases, and concordances, and you'll even find some optional exercises that will guide you into these sources. But these are extras, not necessities. These study guides are comprehensive enough to give you all you need to gain a good, basic understanding of the Bible book being covered and how you can apply its themes and counsel to your life.

A word of warning, though. By itself, Bible study will not

transform your life. It will not give you power, peace, joy, comfort, hope, and a number of other gifts God longs for you to unwrap and enjoy. Through Bible study, you will grow in your understanding of the Lord, His kingdom and your place in it, and those things are essential. But you need more. You need to rely on the Holy Spirit to guide your study and your application of the Bible's truths. He, Jesus promised, was sent to teach us "all things" (John 14:26; cf. 1 Cor. 2:13). So as you use this series to guide you through Scripture, bathe your study time in prayer, asking the Spirit of God to illuminate the text, enlighten your mind, humble your will, and comfort your heart. He will never let you down.

My prayer and goal for you is that as you unwrap and begin to explore God's Book for living His way, the Holy Spirit will fill every fiber of your being with the joy and power God longs to give all His children. So read on. Be diligent. Stay open and submissive to Him. You will not be disappointed. He promises you!

Lesson 1/Introducing Romans

"I'd like to introduce you to . . . ." How many times have those words granted us access to new friends, new business associates or clients, new dates, even future family members? Introductions provide openings into new relationships—relationships that could change our lives with new information, new perceptions, new understandings, new emotions. Sometimes introductions can also open old wounds or create new ones. But no matter what finally results from an introduction, it always promises to give us something new, hopefully something that will enrich us rather than embitter us.

That's certainly true with Romans, the book of the New Testament that has been heralded as the greatest explanation and defense of the central themes of Christianity found anywhere in the Bible. Such giants of the church as Augustine, Martin Luther, John Calvin, and John Wesley were transformed by the message of Romans. In fact, Romans has probably been the most influential book of the Bible in the history of Christianity. This is the book you'll get to know in this study guide. This is the book I want to introduce you to.

But like all good introductions, we have to start with some basics. Intimacy in relationships always begins with some basic information to some important questions: What's your name? Where are you from? What do you do? What are your likes and dislikes? Do you know . . . ? The same is true when you seek to understand a book of the Bible—you start by getting answers to some key questions: Who wrote the book? When and where was it written? To whom was it written? Why was it written in the first place? What is it about? So let's start to get acquainted.

THE AUTHOR

Romans tells us quite a bit about its author. Look up the following passages in Romans and record what you learn about him. Perhaps these questions will help you organize your thoughts:

What was his name and job?
What was he like?
What was important to him? What wasn't?
What brought him pain? joy?
Who impacted his life and in what ways?
Does he mention any travel plans?
What did he want to accomplish? Why?
Does your search indicate anything else about him?

1:1–17

7:13–25

9:1–5

10:1, 2

11:13, 14

15:14—16:27

THE RECIPIENTS

From what you've read in Romans so far, you can tell that it's a letter, sent by the apostle Paul to the Christians in first-century Rome. Most of the books in the New Testament were originally letters, written specifically to address the needs of Christians in certain locales. So these letters were designed to meet people where they lived, hurt, doubted, celebrated, struggled, worried, shared, complained, married, raised families, suffered, and died. They were written to specific people with specific needs, dreams, and wants. They were penned for people like you and me.

What does Paul say in this letter that tells you what the Roman Christians were like? Who were they? Were they mostly of Jewish background? Greek background? What concerned them? How were they doing? What were they expecting? What doctrinal questions might they have had? Were they going astray in any way?

Reread Romans to see what you can discover about this letter's first recipients. If reading the entire book is too much, see what you can find out in the following passages:

1:7–15

2:1–24

4:1, 12

6:1, 2, 11–23

11:13, 17–31

12:1—15:16

16:17–20

Other passages in Scripture also give us information about the Roman believers. Read Acts 2:10, 18:2, and 28:17–28, and record what you find.

BEHIND THE SCENES

In Paul's day all roads led to Rome. Dominating the whole Mediterranean, it was the world's most important and most powerful city during the first century.[1]

It housed a large Jewish population, one almost the size of the one in Jerusalem. So far, the spade of the archaeologist has uncovered six Jewish catacombs (underground burial areas). And from inscriptions in these catacombs, we know there were at least eleven synagogues in Rome.

The Christian population in the city was much smaller, but it was large enough for the Roman Emperor Nero to blame and martyr them for a great fire that destroyed much of Rome in A.D. 64. Christian tradition tells us that the apostles Peter and Paul were two of Nero's victims.[2]

THE PURPOSE

From what you've discovered, you've probably unearthed why Paul put pen to paper and placed this letter in Phoebe's hands so she could deliver it to Rome. There are probably four reasons for Paul's writing Romans. Each group of passages below will help you discover the four reasons. Note that the last two sets of passages don't explicitly say why Paul was writing, but they do suggest why. Observe what they emphasize and question—those factors are the keys to unlock the implicit whys.

1:9–13; 15:22–32 (see Acts 19:21)

1:15–17 (see Jude 3)

1:16; 2:9, 10; 3:1, 2, 9, 29, 30; 9:4, 5; 11:5, 25

2:1–4; 3:9–26; 10:14–21

THE TIME AND PLACE

Where and when Romans was written is not set in concrete, largely because neither is mentioned in the letter itself. But many New Testament scholars think that Corinth is most likely the place where Paul took pen in hand and inked Romans. Phoebe, the letter's courier (Rom. 16:1, 2), was from Cenchrea, which was very close to Corinth. And Paul mentions Gaius as his host (v. 23), who was a very prominent convert of Paul's during his ministry activity in Corinth (1 Cor. 1:14). This means that Paul must have spent enough time in Corinth to compose Romans.

There's good reason to believe this. Most Bible scholars agree that Paul lived in Corinth for three months toward the end of his third missionary journey (Acts 20:3). When he left there, he went to Philippi and joined in the Passover and the Feast of Unleavened Bread (v. 6), which were celebrated in April. So Paul had to have spent the winter months in Corinth, which would have afforded him time to write Romans.

Romans was likely written around A.D. 56, sometime before Paul delivered to Jerusalem a collection for needy Christians (Rom. 15:25–28, 31; 2 Cor. 8; 9). For after this money was safely in Jerusalem, Paul planned on going to Rome to preach and teach and find refreshment, and then press on to Spain to preach the gospel (Rom. 1:10, 11; 15:22–24).

AT A GLANCE

Asia and Greece Revisited (Paul's Third Missionary Journey, Acts 18:23—21:16). Paul visited the churches of Galatia for a third time, and then settled in Ephesus for more than two years. Upon leaving Ephesus, Paul traveled again to Macedonia and Achaia (Greece) for a three-month stay. He returned to Asia by way of Macedonia.

On this third journey Paul wrote 1 Corinthians from Ephesus, 2 Corinthians from Macedonia, and the letter to the Romans from Corinth.[3]

BIBLE EXTRA

If you have a Bible dictionary or encyclopedia, look up the article on Corinth to get an idea of what kind of city it was. Then, if you have time, read 1 Corinthians. You'll see how influential the Corinthian culture was on the believers who tried to live in it. Corinth certainly posed special problems for the early church and Paul's ministry.

THE CONTENT

You'll spend the rest of the study guide digging into the content of Romans, but it's helpful to get an overview of the book before you jump into its details. You may want to read the book and develop a chart of its major themes and divisions. Or maybe you would like to read the text and outline it, giving names or summary statements of its major sections. Whatever approach you take, as you read through the letter, pay special attention to repeated words and phrases. In Romans, some of these are *righteousness, justify(-ied), faith, law, gospel, sin,* and *grace*. Repetition is one way authors highlight their main points.

Below I have given the paragraph breaks indicated in the New King James Version. You may want to read these yourself and supply your own descriptions of their content. Write down anything that will memorialize the passage for you and help you catch the flow of Paul's thought. You might make this a project for this week, reading three chapters daily and developing your own brief paragraph summaries for each day's coverage. A half hour per day will allow this fruitful overview and set you in good stead for the following seasons of study.

1:1–7

1:8–15

1:16, 17

1:18–32

2:1–16

2:17–24

2:25–29

3:1–8

3:9–20

3:21–26

3:27–31

4:1–8

4:9–12

4:13–25

5:1–5

5:6–11

5:12–21

6:1–14

6:15–23

7:1–6

7:7–12

7:13–25

8:1–11

8:12–17

8:18–30

8:31–39

9:1–5

9:6–13

9:14–29

9:30–33

10:1–13

10:14–21

11:1–10

11:11–36

12:1, 2

12:3–8

12:9–21

13:1–7

13:8–10

13:11–14

14:1–13

14:14–23

15:1–6

15:7–13

15:14–21

15:22–33

16:1, 2

16:3–16

16:17–20

16:21–24

16:25–27

FAITH ALIVE

Now that you've gotten acquainted with Romans and its human author, it's time to make some preliminary observations and applications.

What are your first impressions?

What questions has this study raised in your mind so far? You'll want to remember these questions as you work through Romans, so you can find answers to them as you go along.

What do you hope to get out of this study?

In what areas of your life (beliefs, moral standards and conduct, relationships, spiritual gifts, and so on) do you think this study will help you?

Is there anything you have already learned that you would like to take to God in prayer? You can list those items below, then pray about them, or you may even want to include them in a written prayer to the Lord.

1. F. F. Bruce, *Jesus and Paul: Places They Knew* (Nashville, TN: Thomas Nelson Publishers, 1984), 117.

2. Ibid., 123, 125.

3. *Spirit-Filled Life Bible* (Nashville, TN: Thomas Nelson Publishers, 1991), map on 1663.

Lesson 2/God's Great News
(1:1–17)

"Congratulations, it's a baby girl."

"Mom, I did it! I got an 'A' in my math class."

"You can rest at ease now. The surgery was successful."

"Honey, I finally got that raise!"

"You qualified for the loan. The house is now yours."

Sometimes it seems that good things rarely happen to us. Life can be very hard. But then there are those times when things go right, when we get what we have wanted deep inside, when we really receive good news—in fact, great news. A new child enters our lives. One of our kids finally aces that difficult class. A loved one not only makes it through surgery, but the operation begins real healing. That extra income we so desperately needed for so long finally comes through. That dream home—the one with the right amount of space, in just the right neighborhood, in the style we've always wanted— becomes a reality. Those are memory makers, great moments we treasure, times that taste good to palates that too often seem to get only sour, bitter food.

The letter of Romans has this sweet, wondrous taste of greatness. Through the inspiration of the Holy Spirit, the apostle Paul penned an incredible letter of theological depth, moral challenge, and timeless, practical relevance. And all of it wrapped around one grand theme—"the gospel of God" (1:1).

Until now, you've only sampled the food of the gospel as laid out on the table of Romans. But now you'll get your first real serving, and I think you'll find it tastes better than any other great news you've ever received. After all, it comes from the One who brings glad tidings, whose promises never fail, whose faithfulness never falters, whose joy is to give you and me all the bounty of heaven. What better news could we ever want?

"HEREEEEEE'S PAUL!"

When we write letters today, we put our names at the letter's close, but during the first century, the writer would identify himself at the beginning of his correspondence. That's what Paul does here (1:1). He not only gives his name, though. He also identifies himself in three other ways. What are they?

Paul's other letters are listed below. How does he introduce himself in those?

1 Corinthians

2 Corinthians

Galatians

Ephesians

Philippians

Colossians

1 Thessalonians

2 Thessalonians

1 Timothy

2 Timothy

Titus

Philemon

What similarities and differences do you see? What's the most common identifying mark he gives himself? Why do you think he chose that one as primary?

  WORD WEALTH

Bondservant (1:1): This word can be translated *slave* or *servant*. It carries a number of ideas. It could refer to an employee who "could not resign and work for another employer. Highly educated and skilled people, as well as ordinary laborers, were *bondservants*."[1] The word could also refer to a person owned by another. In this instance, Paul might have in mind the Old Testament picture of a slave who out of love makes a lifetime commitment to his master (Ex. 21:2–6). No matter the nuance, the word certainly indicates Paul's loyalty to and service under the Lord Jesus Christ.

Apostle (1:1): An apostle was a member of the early church to whom God gave special authority to proclaim and administer the gospel. The Lord gave His original twelve apostles miraculous gifts and abilities (Matt. 10:1–8) and used some of them to write His words without error (Rom. 2:16; 1 Cor. 14:37; 2 Cor. 13:3; 1 Thess. 2:13; 4:15; 2 Pet. 3:15, 16). To others God also gave the gift of founding and governing churches in a life-multiplying way. Their insights and instructions were key to keeping the church on course (Gal. 1:8, 9; 1 Thess. 4:8; 2 Thess. 3:6, 14).

In the earliest beginnings of the church, not just anyone could be an apostle. A person had to be appointed by God to the task and an eyewitness of the resurrected Christ (Matt. 10:1–8; Acts 1:21–26). Paul qualified on both counts (Acts 9:1–27; 22:6–15; 26:12–20; 1 Cor. 9:1; Gal. 1:1), and he referred to himself as the last of the apostles to see the risen Lord (1 Cor. 15:7, 8).

FAITH ALIVE

How would you describe your relationship to the gospel and to the Lord? Happy? Strained? Marked by assurance? Filled with doubt?

As we'll see below, Paul was confidently unashamed of the gospel (Rom. 1:16). Would you feel comfortable telling people about your commitment to God and His great news for humankind? Record your thoughts, leaving them bare before the One who already knows them. Then consider in prayer any changes you might need to make in your public identification with God and His way of salvation.

 BIBLE EXTRA

With the help of a Bible concordance or Bible dictionary, see if you can list the other apostles of the church. Words you could look up would be *apostle(s), apostleship,* and *disciple(s).* You might also want to find out what happened to these men. Where did they travel? What peoples and nations did they evangelize? What churches did they plant? How did they die? Bible dictionaries and encyclopedias often contain this kind of information. Two other sources you may want to consult are *The Search for the Twelve Apostles,* by William S. McBirnie (Wheaton, IL: Tyndale House Publishers, 1973) and *The Apostles,* by Donald Guthrie (Grand Rapids, MI: Zondervan Publishing House, 1975).

SEPARATED TO REACH OUT

Paul says he was "separated to the gospel of God" (1:1). *Separated* means being set apart *to* something rather than *from* something. Paul was chosen to be committed and dedicated to the gospel, not to be isolated from people or institutions or even from "secular" work. Notice that Paul made tents to support himself and his companions (Acts 20:34; 1 Thess. 2:9; 2 Thess. 3:8); and he also associated with people of different races, religions, and nationalities for the sake of the gospel (Acts 17; Rom. 15:18–21; 1 Cor. 9:19–22). The Pharisees, on the other hand, thought holiness demanded isolation. In fact, even the name *Pharisee* means "separated one" in the sense of being isolated from certain people and things.

FAITH ALIVE

What is your concept of separation? Is it more consistent with Paul's or with the Pharisees'? Is your life defined more by what you don't do and who you don't associate with rather than by what you do and who you reach out to for the gospel's sake?

Sometimes it's hard to be objective about something like this. If you have a close friend or family member in whom you could confide, ask them to help you answer these questions honestly. Regardless, however, observe your words and actions over the next week or so, asking the Holy Spirit to help you see yourself clearly. Then come back to these questions, answer them, and in prayer and consultation with others, seek to make any changes necessary for you to become the loving and outreaching kind of servant God truly desires and whom earnest seekers would be glad to meet.

THE NEWS OF A LIFETIME

By mentioning "the gospel of God" (Rom. 1:1), Paul introduced his letter's major theme. He then went on to describe it briefly. Read verses 1–6 and answer these questions about the gospel:

What's the gospel's ultimate source?

Through whom was it revealed?

Whom is the gospel about?

What does Paul say about this person?

What's said about the Holy Spirit's role?

What benefit is the gospel to believers?

TRAVEL PLANS

After introducing himself and his subject, Paul greets his letter's recipients, the believers (*saints* refers to all Christians, not just to a special group of believers) in ancient Rome (1:7). How does he identify them? What does he hope for them?

WORD WEALTH

Grace (1:7): Throughout Paul's writings, when this word is connected with deity, it refers to God's free love and unmerited favor to human beings, which is given through Jesus Christ and made effective through the ministry of the Holy Spirit.

Peace (1:7): The peace that comes from God is a sense of well-being His children enjoy through the power of His grace.

Here Paul reveals his desire to visit Rome and why he wants to make the trip. But in the context of his laying all this out, we learn a good deal about Paul and his fondness toward the Roman Christians.

What is Paul thankful for? (1:8)

What has Paul been praying for? (1:9, 10)

Why does he want to visit Rome? (1:11–15)

What do these verses tell you about Paul?

 FAITH ALIVE

Reading about Paul's relationship to God can be so convicting! And remember, he was not a supersaint. Though called to minister as an apostle, he still remains without a pedestal. But he served the same Lord we serve—the One who will empower us to godly living just as He empowered Paul.

So take a few moments to consider what Romans 1:8–15 says about Paul's prayer life, his motivations, and his commitment to a body of believers he had never even met. Do these things point toward any changes you would like to make in these areas of *your* life?

GOSPEL ZEAL

If Paul was known for anything, it was for his zeal and boldness (Acts 9:1–30; 13:4–52). And yet, when he refers to the gospel in Romans 1:16, he says, "For I am not ashamed of the gospel of Christ." Why does he let his readers know that he's not ashamed? Was he saying it to allay any thoughts they had about him, or was he seeking to stimulate boldness in their presentation of and commitment to the gospel? Support your answer from the review of Romans you've already done.

Since the gospel is for everyone, why do you think Paul says that it is "for the Jew first"? (1:16) Observe Paul's evangelistic practice and comments before you answer this question (Acts 13:5, 14, 42–52; 14:1–7; 17; 18:1–8, 19; 19:8–10; 28:17–31).

GOSPEL COVERAGE

Today, when most Christians talk about salvation, they mean the *initial* act of placing trust in Jesus as their Savior from sin and as Lord of their life. Is this all Paul had in mind? No. As we'll see in this study of Romans, Paul's understanding of the gospel of salvation is much fuller. Salvation in Christ is total. It covers every aspect of our lives from the moment we trust in Christ throughout the rest of our earthly sojourn and including our entire life of bliss in eternity. It involves salvation from the penalty of sin (which is death here and forever), from the power of sin (which shackles us to death here and forever), and from the presence of sin (which seeks to slap us in the face with death here and forever). The Lord justifies us, freeing us from sin's penalty (Rom. 3:21—5:21); sanctifies us, freeing us from sin's power (6:1—8:16), and glorifies us, freeing us from sin's presence (8:17–30). And He saves all of us—not just our souls or spirits but also our bodies (8:23; 1 Thess. 5:23). He leaves nothing unredeemed. Every bit of us is cleansed, made righteous, healed, transformed. So what the Bible presents is a whole gospel for the whole world that covers wholeness for each person throughout his or her whole life. Now that's a comprehensive health plan!

And how does this great plan become ours? How can we tap into it? There's only one way: by faith (Rom. 1:17). Paul emphasizes this dramatically here, even if his statement is brief. However, to see it clearly, background information is helpful.

The phrase "the righteousness of God" refers to the righteousness that comes from God. Since it comes from Him, it is consistent with His nature and standard. It's a right standing before God that God gives us. And it is this right standing that is revealed—unveiled to us "from faith to faith" (1:17). In other words, it starts by faith and continues by faith. Paul highlights this by quoting Habakkuk 2:4: "The just shall live by faith." This Old Testament passage literally reads, "The righteous person in [or by] his faithfulness [firmness, consistency, belief, faith, steadfastness] shall live!" And *shall live* is virtually synonymous with *shall be saved*. A right relationship with God begins with our exercise of trusting faith in Christ and is maintained by our exercise of trusting faith in Christ. God saves and enables us, yes. Nevertheless, just as we must receive His salvation by faith, we are to grow and persevere in that salvation by faith.

But why must the righteousness that comes from God be accepted by faith? Can we earn it or get it some other way? Not a chance, answers Paul, and he begins to tell us why in the latter half of Romans 1.

---

1. *Spirit-Filled Life Bible* (Nashville, TN: Thomas Nelson Publishers, 1991), 1686, note on 1:1.

Lesson 3/No Excuses
(1:18—2:16)

"Why did you do that, Jimmy?" his mom asked in exasperation. "If I've told you once, I've told you a hundred times not to tease your sister. Why won't you listen to me?"

"But she stuck her tongue out at me! I hate her!!" Jimmy thought his action was fair and just, and he wasn't about to back down.

His mother, though, had finally had enough. "Jimmy, I'm tired of your excuses. If Sara teased you, she was wrong. But that still doesn't give you the right to tease her about the way she looks or about the toys she plays with or her friends or anything else for that matter. Two wrongs don't make a right. When are you going to learn that?"

Jimmy knew what she was talking about. It wasn't new. His mother had told him this repeatedly. But his sister's antics couldn't go unpunished, no matter what his mother said. "What Sara did to me wasn't right either," Jimmy shot back. "You should talk to her, too. I shouldn't be the only one getting in trouble."

"You're right. I *will* talk to her. But that *still* doesn't excuse your behavior."

"But Mom . . . "

"No more buts," his mother said with a reddening face. "I've had it with your excuses. Go to your room until I think of an appropriate punishment."

"But . . . "

"Go! Now!!"

Jimmy crinkled up his face with indignation, spun around, and stormed out of the room, slamming his bedroom door behind him. No matter what his mom said, he still felt he had the right to hassle his sister.

Excuses. Excuses. But even when we get older and sup-posedly should know better, how often do we still pull a 'Jimmy'—try to justify our foolish actions rather than own up to them and seek forgiveness:

- "If my boss only knew how late I stayed up working on that project of his, he wouldn't have gotten angry at me when I skipped work two days last week."
- "Since my wife ignores me on so many other things, I think I should be able to stay out most of the night whenever I feel like it and without telling her."
- "Because he slighted me last time, I don't feel bad that I made him look stupid in front of his friends."
- "When I didn't get that raise and promotion, I decided I would take more sick days just to relax at home and play some extra golf."

We not only make excuses on the human level, but we make them in the spiritual realm, too. Paul confronts us with this fact in Romans 1:18—2:16. And although it may make us feel a bit uncomfortable to face our rationalizations for what they are, we can never enjoy the full benefits of the gospel without having done so. So let's push ahead. The exposure by our heavenly Father may hurt a little, but the incredible heal-ing that can follow will be worth the pain.

WHAT WE ALL KNOW

We saw before that God's righteousness—a right standing before Him that only He can give—comes through the gospel, the good news about salvation by faith through God's Son, Jesus Christ (Rom. 1:16, 17). But this presupposes that we need God's righteousness. Somehow, at sometime, we have gone wrong in our relationship with Him. And we damaged the relationship so badly that we could not repair it. Nothing we could ever do would ever put things right between us and our Creator. So God had to step in and initiate what we couldn't.

What happened? What did the human race do that was so reprehensible to the One who made us? How did we fall out of a right standing with the Lord? Like a prosecuting attorney pressing the case for God, Paul sets out the evidence of our wrongdoing for us to see. The portrait is grim and convincing. It clearly shows that the case against us is ironclad; we are definitely guilty.

What is God angry about? (1:18–21)

Let's analyze these verses a bit more so we don't miss the cause of humankind's separation from God. And this begins with an understanding of some key words and phrases.

 WORD WEALTH

Wrath of God: God's righteous and just anger against anything that twists or distorts His intended purpose and thereby violates and offends His holy, moral character.

Ungodliness: A lack of proper reverence toward God, in terms of rebellion as well as neglect.[1]

Unrighteousness: The injustices perpetrated between human beings in their dealings with each other.

Suppress the truth: "Hold down"—rationalize away or try to excuse or conceal—the true facts about oneself, others, God, or anything else.

Paul says that God is really angry about human "ungodliness and unrighteousness" (1:18). Since ungodliness depicts our relationship with God and unrighteousness describes the way we deal with each other, what do Paul's words tell you about God's concerns? Is our Creator simply upset with the way we treat Him? Why do you think our human relationships matter so much to Him?

BIBLE EXTRA

Exodus 20:1–17 contains the Ten Commandments. Try restating them in your own words. Then consider how many of these commandments deal with our relationship to God and how many concern the way we deal with each other. Do you see any correlation between these commandments and what Paul says in Romans 1:18?

Although the act of suppressing the truth can refer to any and all information about anything and anyone, Paul zeros in on certain truths about God.

What truths about God have people suppressed? (1:20)

How did human beings ever come to know these truths? (1:19, 20)

How obvious are these truths? Can human beings claim ignorance of them? (1:20)

How does this suppression of the truth manifest itself? (1:21–23) Compare your answer to what Paul says in 1:18. Do you see a connection?

Look at verses 21–23 one more time. What's the progression of human suppression? Where does it begin? What does it change about us and how we relate to God?

     FAITH ALIVE

Before going any further, let's turn our attention to some reflective application.

What evidence from the created order do you think demonstrates God's existence and nature?

Has any of this evidence (or any other forms of evidence) been used by the Holy Spirit to help convince you or someone you know of who God is and that He really lives? If so, recount what happened.

From your understanding of Romans 1:18–23, what are the limits of "natural revelation"? In other words, what does the physical creation itself reveal or tell us about the Creator? What is it silent about?

Now check out the passages listed below. Seek to discover how they either confirm or add to what Romans 1:18–23 tells us about natural revelation's limits.

Ps. 19:1–6

Acts 14:17

Acts 17:22–30

Rom. 2:14, 15

Do these passages promote or undermine the idea so popular today that all paths lead to the same God, that all religious perspectives are just different ways of viewing the same ultimate Reality? How might you use these passages to show someone that there's only one God and all contrary God concepts are false?

Idolatry involves replacing the true God with one or more false or demonic gods. And false gods can be mental or metal, animal or human, monetary or technological—indeed, anything that is held up as a substitute for the one real God. What are some idols you see in our society, even among your neighbors? Take a few moments, too, to examine your own heart and mind. Have you erected any false gods? Do you have anything to confess before the Lord?

When God Gives Up

Throughout the rest of Romans 1, Paul wraps his indictment of the human race around a single idea: God giving up people to increased immorality (vv. 24, 26, 28). You see, when people substitute false or demonic gods for the real God—the One we know truly exists and deserves our gratitude and praise—they make their "gods" the standard for what's right and wrong, or true and false. In effect, they have put themselves in the place of God. When this is done by any of us, God permits us to exercise our new station in life; He gives us up to our own foolishness and lets us set our own standards for thought and behavior. The result is a tragic, destructive mess. See for yourself. Read through Romans 1:24–32. In the left-hand column below, record what happens when God gives people up to their idolatrous desires. After you're done, I'll tell you what to do in the right-hand column.

GODLESS ATTRIBUTES	GODLY ATTRIBUTES

Now that you know what characterizes the godless, return to your list to discover what characterizes the godly. How can you find that out? By taking each negative and writing down its positive opposite. For example, the opposite of uncleanness (v. 24) is cleanness, and the positive opposite of (evil) lusts of the heart (v. 24) is good desires of the heart. These positives will help you see what God wants His people to be like in contrast to those who set themselves up against Him by serving false gods.

FAITH ALIVE

Look back through the left-hand column of your chart. Do you know individuals who exhibit any of those characteristics? If so, seek out God in prayer for them, asking Him to help them see their desperate need for Him. Also petition Him to open doors for you lovingly to share the gospel and God's saving power with them.

Now look at the right-hand side of the chart—the side marked "Godly Attributes." Do you see any characteristics that are not part of your life? Don't think just in terms of what other people might see but also of what you know lies in your hidden world, the world of your thoughts and motives. Wherever you fall short, don't despair. God is in the process of purifying and transforming your life. Godliness doesn't come overnight; it takes time—an entire lifetime that will only find completion in heaven. So rather than feeling hopeless, turn to the One who is your hope and ask Him to enable you, through the sanctifying power of His Spirit, to experience a more godly life, especially in those areas where you're struggling. Our heavenly Father is always pleased to grant such requests to His children.

JUDGMENT ON THE JUDGMENTAL

Now Paul turns the case against rebellious humankind to our most common characteristic—self-righteous judging, otherwise known as hypocrisy. But just before he does, he says, "Therefore you are inexcusable" (2:1). The word *therefore* connects what follows it to what precedes it. It's a logical connective, signifying the conclusion of an argument.

See if you can tell how far back in Romans 1 the *therefore* refers to; then briefly summarize Paul's argument so you can more clearly see the force of his conclusion.

Moving on to the subject of hypocrisy, consider Romans 2:1, 2; then from that passage develop a definition of self-righteous judging.

 BIBLE EXTRA

Turn to Matthew 7:1–5. What does Jesus say about hypocrisy? To help you grasp the force of His words, look up the passage in a commentary or find an entry in a Bible dictionary on hypocrisy. See what these resources tell you about Jesus' choice of words in this text, especially the words translated "speck" and "plank." Jesus had a great sense of humor!

What does God think of hypocrisy? (Rom. 2:2, 3)

From verse 4, what do you think God wants us to substitute for a hypocritical attitude?

What will God do to the self-righteous who refuse to change, and on what basis will He judge them? (2:5–9)

What will the repentant receive from God and on what basis? (2:7, 10)

BEHIND THE SCENES

At first glance, verses 7 and 10 seem to teach that salvation is by works. But that cannot be true since it would contradict what Paul himself says elsewhere in Romans (3:21–28; 4:1–8) as well as what the Scriptures teach in other books (Eph. 2:8, 9; Titus 3:5). So what do these two verses teach? Their central point is that God judges impartially. For those who show themselves to be self-centered and doers of evil—in other words, unsaved people—He will judge them appropriately and rightly, pouring out His wrath upon them. Whether they are Jews or Gentiles, it makes no difference. Likewise, those who demonstrate their true nature as children of God by doing good and seeking His kingdom will receive the fruit of their relationship to Him and labor for Him—eternal life. And this they will have regardless of their racial or national status, "For there is no partiality with God" (v. 11). Put another way, we are saved by faith; but living, true faith always produces good works. Otherwise, it is a lifeless, false faith (James 2:14–26).

THE RIGHTEOUS JUDGE OF ALL

From Romans 2:12–16, Paul turns his attention to the presiding Judge and seeks to justify His judgments. The apostle shows that God is just in His judgments by telling us how He judges all impartially.

Does God use the same standard to judge everyone? (2:12–15)

How far does God's judgment go? (2:16)

The last phrase of this passage—"according to my gospel"—proves that the good news includes some bad news. God will judge everyone: their actions, motives, thoughts, words . . . you name it, everything will come under the Judge's all-knowing scrutiny. And none of us, not one single person, will be able to survive His judgment. That's bad, but not all bad. Because those of us who repent and by faith accept His gracious provision of total, eternal forgiveness through Jesus Christ will find the Judge on our side. Rather than His gavel coming down with a sentence of everlasting death, He'll embrace us as a loving Father would His children and give us an incorruptible inheritance of everlasting life with Him. That's good news, even great news! So Paul relates to us *bad* news in order to motivate us toward hearing and receiving the *good* news!

1. Everett F. Harrison, "Romans," in *The Expositor's Bible Commentary*, ed. Frank E. Gaebelein (Grand Rapids, MI: Zondervan Publishing House, 1976), 10:22.

Lesson 4/No Exceptions
(2:17—3:20)

"Dad, it's so unfair!" Jamie almost shouted as he defiantly crossed his arms and slumped down into the couch. "I know I didn't finish my homework, but I've been planning to go to this movie, and now with my friend Sam going, I can go, too."

"But Jamie," his dad calmly countered, "you know the rule: You can't go out until your homework is done."

"I know, I know. But it's ruining my chance to have some fun," retorted Jamie.

"Now, son, this rule is not designed to rob you of fun. If anything, your mother and I set it up so it would free you to have even more fun. It's so much better to go out knowing that your school obligations have been met rather than having them hang over your head, just waiting for you when you return."

"Can't you make an exception this time?" Jamie pleaded. "Pleeease. As soon as I get home, I'll do my homework—I promise."

"No," his dad answered firmly. "We made no exceptions with your two sisters, and we're not about to start now. You have some responsibilities to fulfill before you can go out. If you can't complete them before Sam and his folks leave for the show, then you'll have to pass on the invitation."

"But . . . "

"No exceptions, Jamie. No exceptions."

Has that conversation ever taken place in your home? Maybe it didn't involve an outing to the movies. Perhaps it revolved around a ball game, a neighborhood party, a date, or some other special event. Whatever the case, as the parent, you had to put your foot down, lovingly, of course, but you had to be firm. You knew if you wavered, if you made an exception, an important rule would be undermined. And if the rule went, the relationship between you and your son or daughter might also suffer. So you held your ground, probably to the chagrin of your child.

Did you know our heavenly Father deals with us in a similar way? He sets down certain rules, certain standards, all designed for our welfare and the betterment of His household of believers. As long as we keep them faithfully, we will prosper and so will His household. But when we violate those standards, we hurt ourselves, our Father, and what He wants to do through us to further His kingdom. So how does He respond? Does He just look the other way? Does He excuse our behavior? Does He count us as exceptions to the rule? Not at all. We are all accountable before Him, and He never removes that accountability, sometimes to *our* chagrin.

Let's see what Paul has to say about all this.

NO SPECIAL STATUS ALLOWED

If anyone could have claimed exemption status, the Jews could have. After all, they had been singled out by God for special treatment. They were given the Law. They had the physical sign of God's covenant—circumcision. They were led by God to establish a new land. He gave them victory after victory. He proved through them that He was the one true God, the only one worthy of worship and praise. He gave them miraculous signs of His presence and commitment to them. Yes, they were special. Sure, they had made some mistakes and at times had angered their Lord. But He had promised never to abandon them. Indeed, they were the chosen ones—handpicked by the Creator of all. Surely they would be exempt from His wrath!

Or were they?

Read through Romans 2:17–29. On what were the Jews relying to give them a special standing before God? In what were they boasting?

Now reread those verses, noting *why* the Jews had no special legs to stand on. Why couldn't they claim exemption status?

Paul wraps up his case in Romans 2 by drawing a distinction between outward circumcision and inward circumcision (vv. 25–29). In Paul's day, most Jews had come to believe that only those who had been circumcised in the flesh were saved. This physical religious rite, so they thought, guaranteed a person's entrance into God's everlasting kingdom.[1] Through Paul's pen, however, God revealed a different opinion—one that flatly contradicted this perspective. Take another look at Romans 2:25–29 and see if you can articulate in your own words what God values more than physical circumcision.

FAITH ALIVE

Are you resting your relationship with God on any outward crutches? Church attendance? The exercise of spiritual gifts? The way you dress or behave? Water baptism? Evangelism? Hospital visitation? Singing in the choir? Don't get me wrong. All of these things can be used to God's glory and the spread of His kingdom. But if you trust in them as the Jews trusted in circumcision—to gain you entrance into the blessed state of heavenly bliss—then you need to change your understanding and the source of your trust. Keeping religious rites and going about doing good should be outward expressions of the inward reality of a right standing before God. They are not the means of salvation but the signs of salvation. If you have confused this biblical truth, stop now and turn to God, putting your trust only in Him for your salvation, from its beginning at justification to its end in glorification.

IN GOD'S DEFENSE

Like an astute lawyer, Paul anticipates several objections to what he has just argued. Each criticism comes from his

Jewish readers, and each one puts God on trial. But as we'll see, the Lord's defense is ironclad. And it leads to a declaration that finds all of His accusers—Jew and Gentile alike—guilty.

Read through Romans 3:1–20. As you do, pick out the objections Paul addresses. Hint: They are all in the form of questions. Restate them in your own words, then summarize the answers Paul gives.

Objection 1 (3:1):

Answer 1 (3:2):

Objection 2 (3:3):

Answer 2 (3:4):

Objection 3 (3:5)

Answer 3 (3:6–8):

Objection 4 (3:9):

Answer 4 (3:9–20):

We are not only without excuse before God, but we are all guilty before Him. We have violated His standard of righteousness. Not a single one of us has ever done otherwise. Therefore, law-keeping will not save us; it will not justify us before Him. Instead, the Law exposes us, showing us that we are all sinners, all lawbreakers, all criminals. No exceptions! (All, that is, except one, which we'll learn more about in the next chapter.)

So for now, we need to understand the charge against us, consider the evidence, and weigh the consequences. And when we do, our counterarguments fall to the ground. We are left silent, dumbstruck. Without the Judge's mercy, without the Father's reaching out to His prodigals in love and grace, every one of us is utterly without hope, trapped and condemned in our own sin.

Is there a way out? Have we any hope? Yes, praise God, yes! And it's found in the good news of the gospel, which is about to be unveiled in its pristine, Spirit-enriched, ever dynamic, life-changing beauty.

1.   Everett F. Harrison, "Romans," in *The Expositor's Bible Commentary,* ed. Frank E. Gaebelein (Grand Rapids, MI: Zondervan Publishing House, 1976), 10:34.

Lesson 5/Getting Right with God (3:21—4:25)

Jennie's seventeen-year-old body revealed the deep alienation she felt. Her eyes stared at the floor, not focused on anything, just peering emptily into space. She sat tired and on edge, holding herself with worn hands tucked under her thin arms and with scarred legs tightly crossed. To secure herself even more, she clasped one of her feet firmly behind the other, not allowing any of the room's light to seep through their bond. Slowly, yet with an unbroken rhythm, she gently swayed forward, then backward, as if she were a fragile doll rocking herself to sleep.

Since running away from home, Jennie had seen more of the dark side of life than most people see in a lifetime. It hadn't started out that way. She thought her parents didn't understand her, that they were trying to hold her back from achieving her dream of becoming a famous, wealthy vocal artist. Everyone agreed that she had a good singing voice. So she decided to take her dream and hit the road, looking for fame and fortune.

It was harder than she thought. She got an early break and started singing in small nightclubs and for private and corporate parties. But the jobs were too few and far between. She had to have more money. Besides, the words to the songs began to remind her of all she had left behind. Friendship, love, security, safety. Some pain and misunderstanding, yes, but overall her home environment had been a haven of support and encouragement. Could she have made a mistake? She was still too proud to give a positive answer to that question, so she pushed on, trying to get her career going stronger.

The job offers still came too slowly, but the pain growing inside her seemed to increase ever more rapidly. She tried to ignore the hurt. That didn't work. So she tried to anesthetize it. Her medication became chemical and sexual. For a season, they seemed to help. At least they launched her into a world that allowed her to forget. But reality kept sneaking back, reminding her that she was utterly alone, seemingly forsaken, and a failure.

Eventually, all she had left was roaming the streets. She became one of the homeless statistics, scavenging dumpsters for food and clothing and searching through alleys, doorways, and parks for places to sleep. Her dream was shattered, her security gone, her pride crushed.

Fortunately, her parents had not given up on her. From the day their daughter ran away, they had relentlessly searched for her. Finally, their persistence paid off. Jennie had been found by the police in a neighboring state. The authorities agreed to hold her until her parents arrived.

That's what Jennie was anticipating. She knew her parents were on the way. What would she tell them? How could she face them? What would they say? Would they still love her after all she had done? Jennie was scared, but she had nowhere else to go. Her fight had vanished.

Suddenly, out of the corner of her eye, she saw the only door to her room open. "Jennie," the policewoman quietly said, "someone's here to see you."

Jennie slowly turned her head and saw her mom and dad almost push through the doorway. Arms wrapped around her small, weak frame, and tears wetted her cheeks. She heard no reprimands, no "I told you so's," not a word of condemnation. She felt only forgiveness, gratefulness, and unconditional acceptance. Love had enveloped her. Jennie was finally home. She wept with relief.

Jennie's story is ours as well. We, too, are runaways. Determined to chase our dreams our way, we ran from infinite Love. And like Jennie, we have found that our way is not the better way. Our lives have not improved. Occasionally we might experience a gain; but it's never permanent, and something about it always rings hollow. We know we were meant for something better, much better.

But we'll never find that something on the run. Someday, somehow, we'll have to come to the end of ourselves and turn back to God. When we do, we won't have to go far. We'll discover that He has been pursuing us all along. He longs for us to come back so our relationship with Him will be set right. He won't stick a bony finger in our face and shame us when we turn to Him. On the contrary, the blessings of heaven will pour over us and wrap around us, restoring our hearts, transforming our minds, healing our souls of life's hurts and injustices.

How does this happen? How can we receive such restorative riches? It all begins by getting right with God. That's what Romans 3:21—4:25 is all about.

"BUT NOW..."

In the letter of Romans, the two little words "But now" opening 3:21 introduce the contrast we have longed to hear. After being told what sad shape we're in and how hopeless our situation is, at least if we keep trying to improve it on our own, "But now" sets us up for the solution. These words hark back to Romans 1:18 and the verses that follow through 3:20. For a foretaste of the change we're going to learn about, complete the statements that follow:

THEN . . .	BUT NOW . . .
Received God's_____(1:18)	Receive God's_____(4:6)
Revealed from_____(1:18)	Revealed apart from_____(3:21)
Rejected God by_____	Accept God by _____
_____(1:21)	_____ (3:22)
Condemned by our _____(2:6)	Justified by our _____
	apart from our _____ (3:28)

Now that we've had an appetizer, let's dig into the main course. We're about to feast on the essentials of the gospel.

GOD'S ANSWER TO OUR FAILURE

Since the Law reveals our failure and cannot help us get right before God (Rom. 3:20), what's the answer? It cannot be found in us—we're the problem. So it must come from God. And what is His answer? His righteousness. He grants us a right standing before Him. That's what "the righteousness of God" means in 3:21. And as you've already seen when you filled out the above chart, this position of acceptance comes "apart from the law." This kind of righteousness cannot be earned through obedience to the Law—a Law we don't obey anyway. It can only be received as a gift. Paul tells us that "the Law and the Prophets" are witnesses of this truth (v. 21).

WORD WEALTH

The Law and the Prophets (3:21): This phrase summarizes the content of the entire Old Testament. The Law refers to the Pentateuch—the first five books of the Bible: Genesis, Exodus, Leviticus, Numbers, and Deuteronomy. The Prophets refers to the rest of the Old Testament.

As we'll see, Paul will draw from both sections of the Hebrew Bible to demonstrate that they teach how man can be rightly related to God. In other words, in its basic message, the gospel is nothing new. Righteousness has always been a gift from God; the Scriptures have never taught otherwise.

MAN'S RESPONSE TO GOD'S OFFER

What must we do to receive the gift of righteousness? The answer lies in 3:22.

Faith is trust, reliance. Who is supposed to be the focus of our trust? (v. 22)

Is anyone excluded from this offer? (v. 22)
Why not? (v. 23)

WORD WEALTH

Fall short (3:23): "No one will ever reach God's standard of absolute moral perfection and be worthy of His glory on his own. Therefore, if there is to be any salvation, it must come in another way (see v. 24)."[1]

Did you notice when we can become rightly related to God? Do we have to clean up our lives first? No. Do we need to attend church more regularly or put more in the offering first? No. Do we first need to seek forgiveness from everyone we have ever wronged? No. Our status changes the moment we trust in Jesus Christ. The simple act of faith transfers us from rebellion to righteousness, from enemies of God to children of God, from the condemned to the acquitted.

THE *CHRISTIAN* CENTER

On what basis can God do this for us? The answer centers on Jesus Christ, but it's summarized in four crucial terms.

WORD WEALTH

Justified (3:24): The divine act whereby sinners are declared, not made, righteous.[2]

Grace (3:24): See the definition of this term on page 31.

Redemption (3:24): A release secured by the payment of a price, a ransom.[3]

Propitiation (3:25): The satisfactory answer effected by a sacrificial offering, removing God's wrath and judgment.

With these definitions in mind, turn back to Romans 3, beginning in verse 24, and answer the following questions:

Who justifies us? (v. 24)

What is the basis and means of justification? (v. 24)

What is Jesus Christ's role in all of this? (vv. 24, 25)

 BIBLE EXTRA

The theme of Christ's shedding of blood for our benefit is a central one in the New Testament. Its roots go all the way back to Genesis 3:21, where God spilled the first innocent animal blood to provide clothing for Adam and Eve after they sinned against Him.

See how many Old Testament events you can recall that recount the shedding of innocent blood to deal with someone's wrongdoing. If you're unfamiliar with the Old Testament, you may want to consult a Bible dictionary or Bible encyclopedia and look up the articles on blood, atonement, sacrifices, and the death of Christ.

Then, loaded with this background information, turn to Isaiah 53, Hebrews 9 and 10, and 1 Peter 1:17–19 to see more fully how precious Jesus' shed blood is and what it has accomplished for us.

Why did the Godhead choose to justify us in this way? (vv. 25, 26)

From what you've studied so far, would you agree or disagree with the idea that justification means "God accepts me just as if I had never sinned"? Support your answer, especially drawing on Romans 3:9–26.

THE FATAL ATTITUDE

The entire thrust of Paul's argument up to this point comes to a practical climax in Romans 3:27–31.

Do you recall what people did to reject God and how it impacted them? With deep-seated ingratitude, they turned their backs on Him and arrogantly went their own way (1:21–32). Even the religious Jews, who had all the benefits of a people chosen by God, became boastful about their status, which led them away from the One they claimed to worship and also influenced others to stay away from the true Lord (2:17–24). So what does justification by faith have to do with all this? The answer lies in 3:27–31.

Does justification by faith encourage an arrogant attitude, one that says, "I've arrived, I'm privileged, I've earned my way"? Can it? (vv. 27, 28) Explain your answer.

Who is the justifier, and who can be justified? (vv. 29, 30) Does this allow for boasting?

What do you think Paul means when he says that faith establishes the Law, it doesn't render the Law void—empty or useless or meaningless? (v. 31)

 ### FAITH ALIVE

Arrogance is an insidious thing. It infects everything it touches. It seeps into the bloodstream of gratitude, compliment, accomplishment, or social or religious standing, then slowly contaminates humility while injecting stronger doses of snobbery until its victims really begin to believe that they are better than others and therefore deserve special treatment.

This disease turns especially deadly when it grows in Christians. It sets believers against believers, destroying the church's unity. It turns unbelievers away from God in disgust, for when they see it in Christians it highlights what even they often recognize as petty rivalries, misplaced priorities, backstabbing, and hollow pride.

Has this disease infected your circle of fellowship? your friends or loved ones? yourself? If it has permeated you, you'll likely have a hard time identifying it because you believe you're too good or too spiritual or too together to have such a problem. In fact, that's one of the tell-tale signs of arrogance. A few others are a condescending attitude, prejudice in all forms (religious, doctrinal, racial, national, civic, economic, etc.), difficulty expressing genuine thankfulness to others or requesting help when you need it, a tendency to let everyone know what you've accomplished, a desire to grab the spotlight because you believe you deserve it, and a begrudging attitude toward God and what He does for you. Do any of these characteristics mark you?

You might need to ask someone close to you, someone who will really be honest with you, to help you diagnose your condition. Hint: None of us truly escapes this disease, and the earlier it's detected and routed, the better. So don't treat this issue lightly.

Once you know the level of the disease's advancement, turn to the Lord for forgiveness and transformation. Remember, too, that you'll never accurately diagnose others who may have this disease until you seriously deal with it in yourself.

The heart of hypocrisy is arrogance. And the gospel of justification by faith cuts out hypocrisy's lifeblood.

AN OLD TRUTH THAT STILL BRINGS NEW LIFE

For religious Jews who were trusting in circumcision for their salvation and claiming that Paul was promoting a new doctrine, a new path to God that was really a dead end, Paul dedicated Romans 4. But don't just think this portion of Scripture applies only to those Jewish people. It applies to anyone who thinks that the Old Testament's teaching about salvation is anything other than justification by faith. There's only one way to a right standing before the Lord of all and that's the way of faith apart from works. God has never taught anything else. Never!

 BEHIND THE SCENES

Romans 4 will ring with much more volume if we first consider some background information. Paul anchors justification by faith in the lives and words of two of the greatest and most important Old Testament saints—Abraham and David. Abraham is key because God selected him to be the focal point of His promise to bless all the nations of the earth (Gen. 12:1–3; 15:5, 6). This blessing concerns the redemption of humankind through faith and the recovery of the ability and right to rule over creation. Abraham is "God's revealed example of His plan to eventually reestablish His kingdom's rule in all the Earth through people of His covenant."[4] Abraham is the prototypical *father* of faith. David, on the other hand, is the prototypical *ruler* of faith. Standing as a descendant of Abraham, David was God's choice for king over all of Israel. And God committed to David that his throne would last forever through the rule of a future king, who would be God's very Son (2 Sam. 7:1–17).

Now if Abraham and David accepted the doctrine of justification by faith, if that was how they, too, came into a righteous standing before the Lord, then what makes us think that we can come to God in any other way?

Let's see how Paul develops his case. He begins with Abraham.

What's the question Paul seeks to answer? (4:1)

What's the difference between faith and works? (vv. 2–5)

What led to Abraham's justification? (v. 3; see also Gen. 15:1–6)

WORD WEALTH

Accounted (4:3): To credit something to someone's account. In the case of Abraham and anyone else who believes in God by faith, the Lord credits righteousness to their spiritual account book.

Imputes (4:6): This is the same Greek word translated "accounted" in 4:3, and it has the same meaning in both verses.

In Romans 4:7, 8, Paul quotes David's words from Psalm 32:1, 2. What insight do they provide into the fruit of justification by faith?

What role, if any, did circumcision play in Abraham's justification? (vv. 9–12) What's the significance of your answer for

Paul's argument? for the intended scope of our evangelistic and missionary efforts?

Why can't justification come through the Law rather than through faith? (vv. 13–16)

In whom did Abraham believe, and what does Paul say about Him? (v. 17)

What promise did God make to Abraham, and why was it so incredible to believe it according to human experience? (vv. 18, 20)

What pushed Abraham over the edge to belief rather than to disbelief? (v. 21)

FAITH ALIVE

Do you trust in God's promises as Abraham did? Do you believe what he did about God's ability to accomplish what He promised? If not, open up to the Lord about it. Don't hold back. He can take it. Then ask Him to help you overcome your doubt or anger or whatever is holding you back from really trusting in Him. He wants you to have confidence in Him, so take Him at His word and watch Him work wonders in your life.

What is the significance of Abraham's story for future generations, including us? (vv. 23–25)

BIBLE EXTRA

In building his case for justification by faith, Paul assumes his readers know who Abraham was and what he did. If you don't know his story, you may want to take some time to get acquainted with it. You can read about him in Genesis 11:27—25:11.

If you explore these verses, pay particular attention to the passages that tell of the promise God made to Abraham, how Abraham responded, how and when the promise took effect, and when Abraham was finally circumcised. You will find that Paul's use of Abraham makes his case for justification by faith apart from circumcision absolutely airtight.

FAITH ALIVE

Elsewhere Paul wrote, "All Scripture *is* given by inspiration of God, and *is* profitable for doctrine, for reproof, for correction, for instruction in righteousness, that the man of God may be complete, thoroughly equipped for every good work" (2 Tim. 3:16, 17). When he penned these words, the New Testament was only partially written, so the Scripture Paul largely had in mind was the Old Testament. All of it, he says, not just some of it, is profitable for us. When we read it, study it, meditate on it, pray through it, apply it, minister it to others, we'll build an investment in our lives and the lives of others so incredible that it will last an eternity (cf. Matt. 6:19–21). Just look at the benefits Paul derived from the Old Testament accounts of Abraham and David—the beautiful, treasured doctrine of justification by faith from which all people can benefit if they will only trust in Christ for their salvation.

Have you ignored the Old Testament? Do you think it's irrelevant or that the New Testament supersedes it? Don't miss out on anything God wants to give you. Commit today to balance your study time between the Old and New Testaments. Perhaps that will involve reading one chapter a day out of each Testament, or maybe during your study time through Romans you can commit to spending a little extra time looking up the references given to the Old Testament and pondering them a bit longer than you otherwise would. Whatever approach you take, make it realistic, then stick with it, bathing your time in prayer so the Holy Spirit can teach you, guide you, and strengthen your soul in the everlasting, absolute truth.

1. *Spirit-Filled Life Bible* (Nashville, TN: Thomas Nelson Publishers, 1991), 1691, note on 3:23.

2. Everett F. Harrison, "Romans," in *The Expositor's Bible Commentary,* ed. Frank E. Gaebelein (Grand Rapids, MI: Zondervan Publishing House, 1976), 10:42.

3. John Murray, *The Epistle to the Romans,* in The New International Commentary on the New Testament series (Grand Rapids, MI: William B. Eerdmans Publishing Co., 1965), 1:115–116.

4. *Spirit-Filled Life Bible* 22, "Kingdom Dynamics: Genesis 12:1–3, Prototype 'Kingdom' Person."

Lesson 6/ When Death Brings Life (5:1–21)

Have you ever noticed how Christianity relishes paradox? By *paradox* I don't mean logical contradictions—"square circles," "married bachelors," "one-ended sticks," "two objects identical in every respect." Contradictions have no meaning and no hope of being true. They claim that one thing is true (say, God is always truthful) and its opposite is also true (God is never truthful) at the same time and in the same sense, which is impossible. What they give with the right hand they steal with the left hand, leaving us with absolutely nothing.

Paradoxes, on the other hand, are pregnant with meaning, but they turn our way of thinking upside down. They present us with truths that appear to have no way of being true, but as we ponder them and explore them, we discover they are true, that they provide insight into reality we had never seen before. Consequently, they tend to transform our perspective, and in so doing, they usually change our motivations and the way we behave.

Take, for example, the biblical idea that the best leadership is sacrificial servanthood (Luke 22:24–30; Eph. 5:21–33; 6:5–9). You wouldn't think that to be true given the way many employers treat their employees or the way politicians often wield their powers or the way too many husbands run roughshod over their wives. "Might makes right" is axiomatic throughout much of the world. But Christianity disagrees. We see reality from a different standpoint. Christ's way rightly observes that people will more readily follow leaders who place their followers' needs above their own. Under whom would you rather work—a boss who tries to intimidate you to get the job done or a boss who encourages and enables you to accomplish the task?

Or, consider the paradox of the Christian view of wealth. How do you gain riches? According to the world's approach, you keep what you earn and multiply it in whatever ways will increase your holdings the fastest and easiest. Eventually, you will become wealthy and powerful, able to do what you want, whenever you want, with whomever you want. Christianity pooh-poohs this idea. She sees that this kind of attainment of wealth creates only temporary happiness and constant fear. What you have cannot be really enjoyed because you're always worried you'll lose it somehow. So Christianity in effect says, "Hang on to your holdings loosely, standing ready to use them to reach out to those who are in need, and in so doing, you will invest your wealth in heaven where it cannot dwindle or be taken away at any time, where you will be able to enjoy it for eternity" (see Matt. 6:19–21; Luke 12:13–34; 1 Tim. 6:17–19).

Romans 5 treats us to a paradox similar to these. It talks to us about the event none of us likes to talk about—death. In our society, we do everything we can to remove ourselves from it or to lessen its power to terrorize us. We hire funeral directors to handle all the arrangements for us. We have our loved ones dressed up and made over so they won't look deceased. We often bury our dead without ever seeing them, keeping their caskets closed. We even cover the event with flowers. And we have comfortable synonyms for death: *passed away, gone to their heavenly reward, on to another home.* But once again, Christianity sees things differently. Death is our enemy, yes. Death is not what we were made to experience, yes again. But death is not only our enemy, not only a stranger we must face—it is also a life-giver.

What?! How can that be? What an outrageous idea! Is it, though? Could it be true? Could death, somehow, someway, really bring us life? Romans 5 answers with a resounding "Yes." Let's see how this can be. If true, it will change how we live; it will even change how we face death.

GETTING OUR BEARINGS

Before we go through this tightly reasoned and highly practical passage, we need to get an overview of it. One way to do that is to observe the repeated words; they will reveal many of the chapter's main themes. So in the space below, list those repeated words (ignoring articles such as *a* and *the,* the verb *is,* and connectives such as *and, but, for*). Note how many times they are used and in what verses they appear.

REPEATED WORDS	VERSES/TIMES USED

Now reread Romans 5, but this time note when the following words appear: *therefore, not only that, much more.* They represent key points of transition, connecting preceding and following thoughts. Look up each instance and see if you can summarize the thoughts these connectives look back to and look forward to.

CONNECTIVES	PRECEDING THOUGHT	FOLLOWING THOUGHT
Therefore 5:1		
5:12		
5:18		
Not only that 5:3		
5:11		
Much more 5:10		
5:15		
5:17		
5:20		

You probably noticed that Paul moves back and forth between telling about the blessings of justification and the need for justification. We want to consider each of these aspects more deeply.

JUSTIFICATION'S BLESSINGS

Paul writes, "having been justified by faith, we have . . ." (5:1). Did you notice that Paul's words tell us that the act of being justified is a past fact? He doesn't say, "As you keep on being justified" but "Now that you have been justified." Once we place our trust in Jesus Christ, God declares we are now rightly related to Him. The legal matter of justification is done, over with, fully accomplished. We have been declared righteous, forgiven of our sins. Now the task is to make us righteous, to make our lives fit the declared standing we have before God. And that's the function of sanctification, which we'll see discussed later in Romans.

But for now, Paul wants to tell us what justification brings to us. It not only sets us right with God; at least ten other blessings flow from it, too. See if you can identify them in the following verses from Romans 5.

VERSES	BLESSINGS
1	1.
2	2.
	3.
3, 4	4.
	a.
	b.
	c.
5	5.
	6.
9, 10	7.
11	8.
	9.
17, 21	10.

Let's take a closer look at several key words that will help you get a better handle on what these blessings are all about.

WORD WEALTH

Peace (v. 1): Justification by faith crosses the raging waters of enmity between us and God, building a bridge of restored fellowship and calming the waters.

Rejoice (v. 2): Exult over, boast in, overflowingly enjoy.

Hope (vv. 2, 4, 5): A confident expectation.[1]

Glory of God (v. 2): It is "the outward shining of [God's] inward being,"[2] like the rays of sunlight manifest the presence and power of their source, the sun.

Tribulations (v. 3): Pressures, distresses, hardships, sufferings.

Perseverance (vv. 3, 4): Patient endurance.

Character (v. 4): Quality produced through enduring tribulations.

Love (v. 5): This word translates the Greek term *agape,* which means "an undefeatable benevolence and unconquerable goodwill that always seeks the highest good of the other person, no matter what he does. It is the self-giving love that gives freely without asking anything in return, and [it] does not consider the worth of its object."[3]

Reconciled (v. 10): Through the costly blood Christ shed on the cross, God paved the way for us to return to Him and revel in the fullness of His unconditional love and acceptance. And He did all this even when we were at war with Him, active rebels, shaking our fists in the face of our only real hope for happiness.

FAITH ALIVE

What an awesome array of gifts the Lord has given us. And this is just a partial list of the incredible inheritance that is ours in Christ. Have you ever stopped to consider the abundance you have in the Savior? Take some time to do so now, thanking Him for His lavish goodness.

Now let's go back through different aspects of these verses to gain a clearer vision of what Paul is saying and to apply some important truths.

Through whom can we find peace with God? (v. 1)

What else can we find through this Person, and how can we get it? (v. 2)

Who embodies the "glory of God"? (John 1:14, 18; Heb. 1:2, 3)

When can we expect to see this Person in His glory? (Matt. 16:27; 24:30, 31; Col. 3:4; Titus 2:13)

 FAITH ALIVE

Do you ever meditate on the Second Coming of Jesus Christ? Is it an event you look forward to? Or do you dread it? Perhaps ignore it? Take some time to reflect on the return of Jesus, God's eternal Son, and examine your attitude toward His coming. Even though no human being can know the exact time, day, month, or year of His return (Matt. 24:36; Acts 1:6, 7), we can rest assured that He will come back in glory to glorify His children and punish the sons of wickedness.

Does "glory in tribulations" mean we should praise God because we suffer or because of what suffering can produce in our lives? Support your answer from Romans 5:3–5.

 FAITH ALIVE

What's your response to suffering? Can you think of a time when you were going through hardship and you were able to glory in it? Or perhaps you didn't praise God while you were experiencing tough times, but you did afterward? Regardless of when you turned a thankful heart to God, what led to your praises? Why did you finally find it in your heart to honor the Lord, even in suffering?

Why can our hope be so certain and satisfying? (v. 5)

What does the phrase "in due time" (v. 6) tell you about God's sovereignty—His rule over the world?

What proof does Paul offer for God's love for us? How do we know God really, unconditionally cares for us? (vv. 6–10)

FAITH ALIVE

Is anything going on in your life right now in which you need to see God's sovereign, loving hand at work? Ask Him to show Himself to you, to demonstrate in some tangible way that He is with you and in control of your circumstances for your ultimate good. Don't dictate to Him how He should unveil His involvement to you. Let Him choose the method and the timing. You remain faithful to believe He's at work and continue to watch carefully for signs of His care. Remember, He's the God of surprises, so don't be surprised if He answers your prayer in an unexpected way or at an unusual time.

According to verses 9 and 10, what has Christ done for us through His death and what has He done for us through His life (His resurrection from the dead)?

How should we respond to this incredible demonstration of divine love and grace? (v. 11)

 FAITH ALIVE

It's easy to love someone who loves you back. But what about loving someone who turns on you, who openly defies your standards, slanders you, betrays your loyalty, takes advantage of your generosity, lies to you, steals the credit you deserve, even turns others against you? Could you love someone like that? Would you even sacrifice your life for that person? The Son of God did on behalf of the triune Godhead. Father, Son, and Holy Spirit, loving us infinitely and in unity, willingly carried out a monumental plan to save us rebels from our path of self-destruction. No one can force deity to do anything deity doesn't want to do. And we didn't deserve this unconditional, sacrificial expression of love. We spurned it with everything God had given us! Nevertheless, Love responded to our need, spread His innocent arms wide on a rugged cross, and embraced our punishment so we could enjoy everlasting forgiveness and unending bliss as restored, redeemed citizens of His unimaginable Kingdom.

Who says fairy tales don't come true? They don't come any better than this, because this one is no tale; it's fact, grounded in history and confirmed in our hearts.

Don't wait a moment longer. Turn your eyes toward heaven; and in response to this great act of infinite Love, "rejoice in God through our Lord Jesus Christ . . . by the Holy Spirit who was given to us" (vv. 11, 5).

THE GIFT OF DEATH

Now we come to the heart of Romans 5, perhaps even the crux of the entire letter of Romans. In ten verses (vv. 12–21), Paul summarizes the history of redemption, from the event that made it necessary to the event that stands at its apex. And he does it by comparing the first Adam, who precipitated the Fall of the entire human race, with the Second Adam, who has made it possible for all human beings to enjoy everlasting life with God if they will respond to the Lord by faith. The first Adam brought death through his life; the Second Adam brought life through His death. That's the profound paradox and point of Romans 5.

 BEHIND THE SCENES

This section of Romans 5 builds on the account of the Fall in Genesis 3. From the first two chapters of Genesis, we learn that God created Adam and Eve and placed them in a beautiful setting where they had control over their environment and enjoyed an intimate, harmonious relationship with each other and with their Creator. To keep things this way, all Adam and Eve had to do was obey God's command against eating from the forbidden tree, a violation that would lead to their deaths (Gen. 2:17).

Well, they eventually yielded to temptation, and right away they began to experience the deadly consequences of their disobedience. The open fellowship they had had with God and with each other was lost; now they hid from the Lord and from each other and they tried to blame their wrongful actions on anyone other than themselves (3:7, 8). Adam and Eve also lost control over creation. What had been submissive to their rule became a source of conflict and arduous labor (vv. 17–19). They found themselves ousted from Paradise, barred from natural immortality, and destined to die physically in a hostile world that would now be made up of people who would suffer from a disease far worse than anything man has ever known (vv. 16–24).

The disease? Sin. It infects every human being from the moment of conception, and it always leads to death—alienation from God, from self, from others, from creation, from physical life, and, if one is careless, from spiritual life as well. There's only one cure. Everything else is only a bandage. And the cure is found in Romans 5:12–21.

MEET THE ADAM FAMILY

With this background information in mind, read through Romans 5:12–21 and fill in the chart below. The left column deals with the first Adam, the one who disobeyed his Creator in Genesis 3. The right column concerns the Second Adam, the One who has never disobeyed His heavenly Father. Note the similarities and differences. You may discover some real surprises.

THE FIRST ADAM   THE SECOND ADAM

Similarities

Differences

Let's take a closer look at these verses in light of some of the discoveries you made in the chart above. Feel free to check back over verses 12 through 21 as you consider the following questions.

Did you notice that Paul refers to Adam and to Jesus as human beings? What did Jesus do as a man that Adam did not do? What were the consequences of Jesus' actions as opposed to Adam's?

     BIBLE EXTRA

Paul refers to Adam as a "type" of Christ. The term *type* refers to a "form, figure, pattern, example." When types are found in Scripture, they are historical persons, events, things, or institutions that prefigure or foreshadow persons, events, things, or institutions yet to come in God's plan. Types, then, are prophetic, predictive. They depict not only someone or something that has already played a role in history but someone or something that *will yet* play a role in history. In Romans 5, Paul uses Adam as a prefigurement of Jesus Christ. In certain ways, Adam and his actions foretell certain truths about Jesus Christ. But these truths, as Paul lays them out, are negative on Adam's side but positive on Jesus' side. In other words, Adam is a type of Christ because he failed to do in a perfect environment what Jesus did successfully in a sin-ridden environment. So Paul contrasts Adam and Jesus far more than he compares them.

Over the centuries of biblical studies, many other types have been found in the Bible. Below are pairs of scriptures that give some of the types that have been identified. You may want to look these up and reap for yourself the insight they contain.

OLD TESTAMENT TYPE	NEW TESTAMENT FULFILLMENT
Gen. 7; 8	1 Pet. 3:20, 21
Gen. 15:1–6	Rom. 4:16–25
Ex. 20:8–11	Heb. 4:3–10
Lev. 17:11	1 Pet. 1:18, 19
Num. 12:7	Heb. 3:1–6
Num. 21:4–9	John 3:14, 15
Jon. 1; 2	Matt. 12:39, 40

Of course, there are many other types in Scripture. If you want to discover more of them and learn how to find and interpret them, I suggest you consult these sources: *Protestant Biblical Interpretation,* by Bernard Ramm, 3rd ed. (Grand Rapids, MI: Baker Book House, 1970); *Principles of Biblical Interpretation,* by L. Berkhof (Grand Rapids, MI: Baker Book House, 1950); *How to Read Prophecy,* by Joel B. Green (Downers Grove, IL: InterVarsity Press, 1984); *Encyclopedia of Biblical Prophecy,* by J. Barton Payne (New York, NY: Harper & Row, 1973).

Granting both Adam and Jesus were true human beings, does Paul say anything in Romans 5:12–22 that suggests Jesus was also more than human?

What does Paul say about the Law in this section of Romans? What role did it play in relationship to sin and redemption? (vv. 13, 20, 21)

What balanced out the Law and its purpose? (v. 20) Since the Law and the gospel have the same source—the Lord—what does your answer tell you about God? How, if in any way, should you respond differently to Him as a result of this discovery?

 FAITH ALIVE

Now that you've come to the end of this chapter, take some time to review the truths you've uncovered, then reflect on how you can begin to make them a part of your life this week. If you need some guidance, try relating your discoveries by completing the statements below. They will help you begin to apply more specifically what you have learned.

"Some truths I discovered in this chapter that I want to make a part of my everyday life are":

"This week, I will begin to apply these truths to the following areas of my life in these ways":

My relationship to God:

My relationships to loved ones:

My self-development, including my self-image:

My outreach to unbelievers:

My fellowship with believers:

My attitude toward material possessions and desires:

My perspective and attitude toward death:

1. John R. W. Stott, *Men Made New* (Downers Grove, IL: InterVarsity Press, 1966), 13.
2. *Spirit-Filled Life Bible* (Nashville, TN: Thomas Nelson Publishers, 1991), 1694, note on 5:2.
3. Ibid., "Word Wealth: 5:5 love."

Lesson 7/Free at Last!
(6:1—7:25)

People move away from their homelands looking for it, sometimes leaving friends and family behind. Others blaze new trails, facing unknown dangers in the pursuit of it. Many fight against addictive demons—drugs, alcohol, food, workaholism, smoking, perfectionism, pornography—just for a taste of it. Far too many die on native or foreign soil in defense of it. More and more people seek to find it in financial independence. And untold numbers have turned to every kind of religion imaginable striving to experience it.

Statues are erected in honor of it. Music and paintings are commissioned to celebrate it. Armies are trained to fight for it. Schools teach students to respect it. Riots break out and demonstrators march to voice frustration over not having it. Support groups gather to discover and nurture it. Religious leaders and their followers pray for it.

Countries rise and fall . . . political ideologies come and go . . . religious leaders wax and wane . . . families pull together and split apart . . . businesses flourish and go bankrupt . . . all because of it.

What could be so highly treasured? so honored?

Freedom!

We all want it, even when we fear it. We were created to enjoy it, to experience nothing less. But in the far reaches of our history, we lost it. The freedom we knew under God became a dream engulfed by a nightmare. That God-given ability to satisfy the desires of our heart in ways that were always pleasing to our Creator became distorted, strained, twisted. We still wanted our freedom, though, but we kept going after it in the wrong ways. So we became slaves—slaves to cravings that drew us further away from God, from the One who lovingly created us free to serve Him. Traces of our original dream still linger; deep within our souls we still hunger for it. So we still try to make it come true. But we'll never find it apart from God.

Paul realizes these facts, and so far in Romans he has pointed the way to our regaining our freedom. But it's here, in Romans 6:1—7:25, that our guide takes us into the very heart of what he has been leading us to. Here he shouts to us: "Herein lies true freedom! Listen well." Let's do just that.

DEAD TO LIVE

True freedom has its critics—people who think that if you give people to much leeway, they will always take it to extremes and fall into immorality. Anticipating just such a backlash, beginning in Romans 6, Paul imagines a critic standing in the crowd ready to pounce on him because of what he wrote in the last verses of Romans 5: "Moreover the law entered that the offense might abound. But where sin abounded, grace abounded much more, so that as sin reigned in death, even so grace might reign through righteousness to eternal life through Jesus Christ our Lord" (vv. 20, 21). The critic rises up against Paul and tries to trap him. What problem does he see that could topple Paul's argument? (6:1) Try to state it in your own words.

Paul begins his answer to his critic with a statement of denial and two questions (vv. 2, 3). See if you can paraphrase his response.

Let's reflect on all this for a moment. What does it mean to die to sin? Does it mean that we are as dead to sin as a corpse is to breathing? Just as a corpse is absolutely unable to breathe air, are Christians unable to sin? Is that interpretation supported or refuted by Romans 6:12–14?

Given what Paul says in Romans 6, he views death as the separation of a relationship rather than the extinction of the body or the soul or the self. What verses in this chapter do you see indicating that?

What difference does this understanding of death play in Paul's response to his imaginary critic? Does it allow the possibility that we can still sin even though we are saved? Does it leave room for the possibility that we can choose to renew our relationship with sin even though we should not?

Paul also talks about our being "baptized into Christ Jesus," being "baptized into His death" (v. 3), being "buried with Him through baptism into death" (v. 4). What do you think He means by these phrases? Is he referring to water baptism as the means of our identification and union with Christ or as a symbol—a public proclamation—of these realities? or both? or to something else altogether? What passages, especially in Romans, would you cite to support your answer? You may want to consult a Bible dictionary or a commentary to help you answer these questions.

How does our union with Christ in His death separate us from sin's power and bring us freedom? (vv. 6, 7)

    WORD WEALTH

Our old man (v. 6): "Our preconversion life, what we were before becoming Christians under the unrestrained dominion of the flesh (sin nature)."[1]

Body of sin (v. 6): This does not refer to just our physical bodies but includes our emotions, will, mind, body—everything about us that is dominated by sin's power.

Done away with (v. 6): This means that the power sin has wielded over our lives is made inoperative, defeated, deprived of power, but it does not mean that sin's power becomes extinct or is totally destroyed.

With our pre-Christian life crucified and sin's dominating power over our lives short-circuited, what are we no longer? And what have we become or will we one day become? Read verses 2–10 with these questions in mind and fill in the following chart with your answers.

BEFORE CHRIST	AFTER CHRIST

What role does Jesus' resurrection play in all this? What does it secure for us? (vv. 4, 5, 8–10)

ALIVE TO DIE

We have discovered some great truths about our new life in Christ and how we can know they are true. But how can they become realities in our daily lives? After all, we still fall prey to temptation. We still feel sin's tug even though its power does not hold sway over us as it used to. How do we deal with this? Paul tells us in verses 11–23, giving us three steps we must take so we can experience our new freedom. The first step begins with what sounds like a term out of the old American west—*reckon.*

STEP 1

In verse 11 *reckon* does not mean "I guess I'll go to town for some grub." The Greek verb translated *reckon* means "to consider, to take into account." And its verb tense coupled with its meaning gives us the idea of "continually considering, constantly taking into account." And what should we keep on considering? Two truths—one positive and the other negative (v. 11):

The negative truth:

The positive truth:

In whom are we to reckon these truths? In whom are they valid and operative?

Why do you think that's significant?

FAITH ALIVE

Think about what you can begin doing this week that will help you continually consider your death to sin and aliveness to God in Christ Jesus. What ideas come to mind? Commit today to start putting them into practice.

STEP 2

In verses 12–14, Paul gives us the second step to dealing with sin's power. This step includes two don'ts and two dos:

Don't

Don't

Do

Do

What do these don'ts and dos mean? If you haven't already done so, try to restate them below in your own words.

Look at these commands again. *Who* is told to do or stop doing something? _____ What does that tell you about our abilities and responsibilities in Christ?

The essence of the second step is found in the Greek word translated *present*. In other words, Paul calls on us to submit ourselves to God as resurrected from sin's penalty and power to become His servants of righteous living. We don't serve sin anymore; sin is no longer our master. God is our new master, and we are His servants because of our identification and union with His Son through His crucifixion, death, burial, and resurrection. And as His servants, we are called on to counter sin's advances with the good offense of godly living.[2]

STEP 3

At the beginning of verses 15–23, Paul's imaginary critic comes forward again with another charge meant to topple Paul's case for grace and freedom. The charge builds off of Paul's statement in verse 14 that "sin shall not have dominion over you, for you are not under law but under grace." "Oh yeah?" sounds the critic. "If that's so, should we go ahead and sin anyway? After all, where there's no law, there's no restraint, right?" (v. 15).

Once again, Paul answers with a resounding "No" (v. 15) and counters with a question followed by a more lengthy response. His reply gives us the third step in our fight against sin's power in our lives. It begins with the realization that we have a choice to make. What is this choice? The answer lies in verse 16.

Since we have changed management—we are no longer under sin's dominion but under God's—what should we do?

Should we serve sin, our old master, or should we serve God, our new Master? (vv. 17–19)

In what should our service to God consist? What does it lead to as opposed to what our service to sin led to? (vv. 19–23)

Although Paul uses the imagery of slavery to talk about our service to God in Christ as well as our service to sin apart from Christ, what are the differences between slavery to God and slavery to sin? Some of these differences are brought out in Romans 4—6, but you may be able to think of some others as well. Fill in the following chart with your discoveries:

DIFFERENCES BETWEEN . . .

SLAVERY TO SIN	SLAVERY TO GOD

Make a comparison of Romans 6:16–18 and Galatians 4:6–9, noting how Christ's program of deliverance breaks bondage to *both* our flesh (selfish desires and self-will) and the Devil (any unbroken stronghold in our lives *now*, which relates to issues *past* but whose torment is ready to be broken as truth makes us free!).

What sole survival power has this "foreign" master? (Rom. 6:16; Gal. 4:9)

What pattern pursued brings deliverance? (Rom. 6:17; Gal. 4:6; 5:1, 16)

What contrast of possibilities is shown?

Positive (Rom. 6:18)

Negative (Gal. 4:9)

Comment on the comparative terms that show the relationship we now have and how each points to new liberty in Christ.

Romans 6:16 (slaves)

Galatians 4:7 (sons)

FAITH ALIVE

The detriments of serving sin and the benefits of serving God are clear. Can you think of any reasons why you might choose slavery to sin over freedom in Christ? Do those reasons outweigh the eternal consequences of remaining under sin's dominion?

What are the areas in your life where sin still has a stranglehold? List each one, then turn to God, asking Him to forgive your sin and help you initiate a plan that will break sin's hold over these aspects of your life. Remember, freedom is yours *in Christ*, so don't leave Him out of your plan.

FREED FROM THE LAW, TOO

If you'll recall, earlier in Romans Paul pointed out that the Law revealed and even enticed our sin. It showed us how guilty we really were and therefore condemned us to death while also pointing us to the Savior. So what about the Law now? After we place our trust in Christ, are we still condemned by the Law? Does it still have the same role in our lives as it once did? Not at all. We have been set free from the Law, not just from sin's power and penalty. The basic principle undergirding Paul's thought on this is stated in 7:1. What is that principle?

Paul goes on to illustrate that principle with an example drawn from what the Law says about marriage and remarriage (vv. 2, 3). Summarize his example in your own words:

What does Paul's principle and illustration have to do with our relationship to Christ? (v. 4)

In our preconversion state, how did the Law impact us? (v. 5)

Why has God seen fit to deliver us from the Law? Put another way, now that He has set us free from the Law, what are we to do with our freedom? (v. 6)

 FAITH ALIVE

God is in the guiding business. He wants us to look to Him for answers and direction. So do that now, asking Him to show you what you can do to "serve in the newness of the Spirit and not *in* the oldness of the letter" (v. 6).

 BIBLE EXTRA

The idea that we are free from the Law raises questions about whether we have been freed from obeying any aspect of the Law. For instance, are we still responsible to regard and obey the Ten Commandments? Of course! But what about the ordinances referring to animal sacrifices and other forms of worship? Are we exempt from those? How do those ordinances differ from the commands and promises concerning tithing and the social responsibility to seek justice for the underprivileged or wronged? How far, exactly, does our "freedom" from the Law extend?

This issue is important and not unresolvable. If you would like to explore for yourself, here are some resources you may want to consult: From Scripture, check out Matthew 5:17–48; Romans 3:31; 7:12, 14, 25; 8:4; 13:8–10; Galatians 3:19–25; Hebrews 10:1–22; James 1:21—2:26; 1 John 5:1–5. Another good source is *A Theology of the New Testament,* by George Eldon Ladd (Grand Rapids, MI: William B. Eerdmans, 1974), ch. 35.

THE LAW ON TRIAL

Once again, Paul's imaginary critic raises another objection. Paul has said several things about the Law that could lead one to think that the Law was evil or sinful (see 3:20; 5:20; 7:4–6). But did Paul believe this? What relationship did he see between the Law and sin? (7:7–12)

If the Law itself is not sinful but is good, is it still the cause of death to us? (v. 13) "Certainly not!" exclaims Paul. Then what is? (v. 13)

THE WAR WITHIN

Before we go any further, we need to look at a controversy that has arisen over Romans 7:7–25. The dispute revolves around differences in interpretation of these verses. Before I get into the details, however, take a few minutes to read 7:14–25 for yourself.

Now let me tell you what the dispute is all about. The issue revolves around what Paul is describing: (1) Do these verses describe Paul's experience before he became a Christian? (2) Or do they tell us what he is experiencing as a believer? (3) Or do they reveal how people in general try to live when they attempt to attain righteousness in their own strength and apart from the Holy Spirit's work? (4) Or do these verses describe a carnal, substandard Christian life? By referring to Romans, let's see if we can resolve this controversy, at least to some degree.

Reread 7:7–25 and circle all the personal pronouns (I, me, myself, you, we, us). To whom does Paul primarily refer?

What indication, if any, do these verses give that they refer to more than just Paul's experience?

Verses 7–13 are in the past tense; Paul is looking backward, into the past, not forward or to today as he does in verses 14–25. Could that indicate that verses 7–13 deal with his days as an unbelieving Pharisee and that verses 14–25 concern his experience as a Christian?

What is it, exactly, that Paul struggles with? What is the conflict between? (vv. 15–23)

 ## FAITH ALIVE

Do you ever experience what Paul is describing? Do other believers you know share that experience, too? How would you state what Paul is talking about in light of your own experience?

Many find great encouragement in Paul's testimony of his apparent struggle to overcome—and his evident victory (Rom. 8). Paul describes a desperate situation, an experience filled with frustration and a sense of hopelessness. Even he cries out in despair after recounting it (v. 24). Is it totally bleak? Is there really no hope? Absolutely not! We can experience victory. How? The answer lies in verses 24, 25:

As we'll discover in Romans 8, though, this is just the first part of the answer. We really are free from sin's dominion, but we can't enjoy that freedom in our own power. We need help. Who will come to our rescue? God will, but how? That's the question Paul answers in chapter 8.

1. *Spirit-Filled Life Bible* (Nashville, TN: Thomas Nelson Publishers, 1991), 1696, note on 6:6.

2. Charles R. Swindoll, *Learning to Walk by Grace: A Study of Romans 6—11,* ed. Bill Watkins (Fullerton, CA: Insight for Living, 1985), 3.

Lesson 8/Heirs of Glory
(8:1–39)

If you've ever lost a loved one, you know how hard handling death can be. Words can't adequately describe the sense of incredible pain and utter loneliness death leaves in its wake. The loved ones left behind aren't called the survivors for nothing. No other event in life is harder to endure.

One thing, however, that can take a little bit of the edge off of the sharpness of death is the inheritance the deceased leaves behind. Whether it's great financial wealth or a small bank account, awards and trophies or words of deep comfort and encouragement, an inheritance is a treasure to those who receive it. It's a legacy, a memorial, a sign of love from the one who has gone ahead of us.

Did you know that if you're a Christian, you have been given an inheritance? That's right. Jesus Christ so loved you and me that He not only set us free but left us an inheritance that can never be matched, much less superseded. It's a wonderful, incredible, absolutely glorious demonstration of His infinite, unconditional love for us.

Are you curious as to what it is? Do you have any idea when you will receive it and how? Is there any way you can lose it? Would you like to learn more about it? Then read on. Paul has much to teach us in Romans 8 about this marvelous gift. And it all hinges on the Third Person of the Trinity, the Holy Spirit.

FEATURES TO REMEMBER

Romans 8 has many striking features. Before we jump into the details of this chapter, let's spend some time looking for some of these features.

First, read through Romans 8, noting what each member of the Trinity is called and does. Put your findings in the following chart:

THE TRINITY IN ROMANS 8

FATHER (mostly called "God")	SON	HOLY SPIRIT

Now go back through Romans 8 to see what it says about those who are in Christ. What are believers called? What has been done for them? What is still in store for them? What can they count on? Record your answers below.

BELIEVERS IN ROMANS 8

Descriptions Or Names	Past Status	Present Status	Future Situation	Resources Available

Did this overview raise any questions you want to explore later? Go ahead and list those questions here.

WELCOME, HOLY SPIRIT!

Toward the end of Romans 7, Paul almost ended on a note of despair. How could he possibly fight and win the war raging within him between the old man dominated by sin and the new man hooked on good? Answer? Only "through Jesus Christ our Lord" does Paul or any believer have a fighting chance (7:25). But what is it that Christ brings us that enables us to fight and win the war within? Answer? The Holy Spirit! What Jesus promised in John 14 and Acts 1 and came as the beginning of the fulfillment of that promise in Acts 2 is the centerpiece of Paul's answer in Romans 8. Apart from the

Holy Spirit's work in our lives, we would be in deep trouble. It would be utterly impossible for anyone to live the Christian life, because only God's Spirit makes such a life possible through His enabling power and other resources. Without the Holy Spirit, sin would continue to have the upper hand in our lives. Let's see how all this works.

What do those of us who are "in Christ" not have anymore? (8:1)

What does that mean?

 FAITH ALIVE

Knowing we are no longer condemned and feeling as if that's true can sometimes be two very different things. Are you a believer? If so, do you ever feel like you're under the condemning hand of God? In this case, you need to ignore your feelings and let the truth of your new relationship with Him take hold. Commit Romans 8:1 to memory or write it on cards and stick them in several places where you will see them often. Let this truth penetrate to the depths of your being. Believe me, it will refresh your soul and transform your feelings.

Paul assumes that "those who are in Christ" live ("walk") according to whom? (v. 1)

What other way of living is there?

Is it meant for Christians?

Who has set us free, from what have we been liberated, and how was our freedom secured? (vv. 2–4)

NOT ALL LIFE-STYLES ARE WORTH LIVING

In verses 5–11, Paul contrasts life according to the flesh and life according to the Spirit. See if you can identify the contrasting characteristics of these two life-styles.

CONTRASTING LIFE-STYLES

THE FLESHLY LIFE	THE SPIRITUAL LIFE

FAITH ALIVE

We all know our capacity to allow either our own flesh or the Holy Spirit to gain the upper hand in our lives. What are the different ways the flesh shows up in your life?

When can you tell the Holy Spirit is having His way?

Ask the Holy Spirit to help you submit more to His guiding hand so you can strip the flesh of its destructive influence in your life.

As believers who have the Holy Spirit dwelling in us, what obligation do we have and to whom? (v. 12)

What is the outcome of the life-style options before us? (v. 13)

What does it mean to "put to death the deeds of the body"? (v. 13) Draw on your understanding of what Paul has already said in Romans to answer this question (Rom. 6:1–18).

 FAITH ALIVE

Now take your understanding of "put to death the deeds of the body" and commit to turning to the Holy Spirit daily, petitioning Him to inform you about how to do this and then to enable you to follow through.

Remember, this is a prayer request the Spirit will always answer because it clearly accords with God's will. So if you ever fall prey to the deeds of your sin nature, don't blame that on the Spirit. He will always meet your need in this area. Any failures you experience will be your responsibility, not His.

HEIRS OF PROMISE

In verses 14–17, we learn some startling truths about ourselves as believers and the Holy Spirit as our . . . well, let's see.

What do verses 14–17 tell us about what the Holy Spirit does for us and through us?

What do these verses tell us about the closeness of our relationship to God as a consequence of the Spirit's work?

WORD WEALTH

Abba (v. 15): This term is Aramaic, which is probably the language Jesus spoke, and it means "father, daddy." It is an expression of intimacy between a child and his or her father.

FAITH ALIVE

How does the Spirit lead us? And how can we be sure that the guidance we sense is from the Spirit and not from our own desires? Think about the times you have sensed the Spirit's guiding hand. Were you right? Was the Spirit doing the directing? How did you know?

How does the Spirit bear witness with our spirit that we really are God's children?

As sons of God, we are "heirs of God and joint heirs with Christ" (v. 17). Although Paul will tell us later more about what we will inherit, in verse 17 he gives us a hint. What is that hint?

Although our inheritance appears to be conditional on whether we suffer with Christ, that's not what the word *if* means in verse 17. The idea may be better expressed as "*Since* we suffer" rather than "if."[1]

Does the idea of our suffering with Jesus fit with what Scripture says elsewhere about what His disciples will experience? Here are a few passages you might want to consult: Matthew 5:11, 12; Mark 8:34–38; John 15:18–21; 16:33; Acts 14:21, 22; 1 Peter 3:13–17; 4:12–19.

Sufferings are shown here to refer to vastly greater issues than temporary difficulty or pain. The whole scope of spiritual warfare, persecution, and oppression is in focus. As Paul thinks about our present sufferings, what does he say about how they compare to our inheritance? (v. 18)

What are the differences Paul brings out between our present sufferings and our future glory? List as many as you can find.

AN INHERITANCE TO DIE FOR

What are the various ways Paul describes our coming glory in verses 17–39?

What assurance do we have that this glorious future will really be ours? (vv. 17–39)

Paul ties the creation's future to ours (vv. 19–22). What is the connection? Why is the creation in bondage and what does its longing for redemption have to do with ours? You may need to read Genesis 1—3 and reread Romans 5 for more help in answering these questions.

 FAITH ALIVE

It's hard to read a newspaper or a magazine or watch the news without hearing something about the environment. Ecology is a hot item these days. In God's Word, however, ecology has always been important. The Genesis mandate (Gen. 1; 2) to subdue and care for the earth has never been revoked by the Lord. And as we can see from Romans 8, God has the entire creation's best interest in mind. He cares for all of creation, not just for His human creatures.

What are you doing for the environment? How are you showing a caring heart for it—a concern that mirrors God's very own? Consider three things you can start doing this week that will provide for the care of the environment.

SPIRIT AT WORK

In verses 23–27, we really see some of the richness of the Spirit's work in our lives. He is actively at work in our behalf. Summarize in your own words what these verses tell us about the Spirit's ministry to us, in us, and for us.

What a comfort it is to see how the Holy Spirit both assists our intercession *and* Himself intercedes for us before the Father. Notice what His intercession is "according to." Is it designed to fit with our will or with God's? (v. 27) According to verse 28, what is the benefit of that kind of intercession for us? Can you see how verse 28 depends for its fulfillment upon our allowing the Holy Spirit to intercede through us in the face of difficult situations? Comment on this "condition" to the promise and what it means for you.

 FAITH ALIVE

How can "prayer in the Spirit" help you to pray for God's will to be done? Are you confident that God's will for your life is always better than yours? Reflect on these questions; and commit to allowing the Holy Spirit to regularly assist you in prayers, putting your prayer life in His hands rather than trying to master every question in your own wisdom.

Compare Romans 8:26, 27 with 1 Corinthians 14:15, Ephesians 6:18, and Jude 20. What benefits do you find through Holy Spirit-assisted prayer?

NOTHING LEFT TO CHANCE

Just as Holy Spirit-empowered prayer is the condition for "all things working together for good," what is the guarantee or power that assures this "good" for those who love God? (vv. 29, 30)

 WORD WEALTH

Foreknew (v. 29): The aspect of God's omniscience whereby He knows the future of all things and events before they ever come to be.

Predestined (v. 29): The act of God's will whereby He determines what will take place and how it will occur, whether through His free will or His permission of the free will of others.

Called (v. 30): God's invitation to come to Him by faith.

Justified (v. 30): The act of God whereby He declares believing sinners righteous and as now without a record of past sin.

Glorified (v. 30): Our future state of heavenly perfection and bliss; our ultimate inheritance. It's the promised culmination of the sanctification process begun after we place our faith in Christ. And it's so certain that Paul can refer to it in the past tense.

With such an incredible plan and guarantee that it will be carried out, Paul raises five questions, all designed to give us an unshakable security in our present trials and future destiny (vv. 31–39). What are these questions, and what answers can possibly be given to them?

Question 1:

Answer?

Question 2:

Answer?

Question 3:

Answer?

Question 4:

Answer?

Question 5:

Answer?

We are as secure as secure can be—now and forever. The God of the entire universe—the greatest power and lover of all—gives it His perfect guarantee, and He is never wrong and He cannot lie (Titus 1:2). Now that's something to get excited about!

1. C. E. B. Cranfield, *A Critical and Exegetical Commentary on the Epistle to the Romans,* The International Critical Commentary (Edinburgh: T. & T. Clarke Limited, 1982), 1:407–408.

Lesson 9 / Promises That Never Fail
(9:1—11:36)

- "You said you were going to fix that faucet yesterday, and the week before that you promised to fix it, too. When are you really going to do it?"

- "I've heard that too many times before. Face it, you're not going to change now or ever!"

- "'I'm sorry, I'm sorry, I'm sorry.' I'm so sick of hearing how sorry you are. I just want you to follow through on what you say you will do—just once!"

How many times has someone promised to do something for you, only never to deliver, at least not at the right time. How frustrating that is, especially when you're really counting on that person's coming through. Of course, not one of us has ever fulfilled all our promises to anyone, but that doesn't discount the fact that promises unkept create anxiety, anger, guilt, frustration, and disappointment. No one likes to break a promise, but everyone hates it when promises made to them are violated. Nowhere is this more clearly seen than in a person's relationship to God.

Have you ever met someone who believed God had failed her? Is she forgiving or understanding about it? Not a chance. She's bitter, hostile, even revengeful toward God. She wants nothing to do with Him, unless she can figure out a way to get back at Him.

Have you ever felt that toward God? Have you ever believed that He let you down—that His promises meant nothing, that He was only playing with your mind and emotions, that He never intended to follow through on what He said He would do? If so, you're not alone. At various times in human history, even some of the men and women in Scripture doubted God's promises (Gen. 18:9–15; Job 16:6–17; Luke 1:18–20).

But if Scripture records anything, it records hundreds upon hundreds of instances where God promised to do something and then did it. So unfailingly consistent has He been that the biblical writers remark about it frequently, even referring to the Lord as the One who is ever faithful, even when we are not (Ps. 119:89–91; Hos. 11:12; 1 Thess. 5:24; 2 Tim. 2:13). Only God always keeps His promises, but this doesn't stop us from doubting Him.

Paul understands that. And he knows that in spite of all the evidence he has amassed for the truth that God works all things for the benefit of believers, the question is raised, What about God's promises to His chosen seed—the natural descendants of Abraham, the Jewish people? Will He still keep His promises to them, especially now that He has included the Gentiles in His plan in a way that seemed to many Jews in Paul's day to have overlooked if not omitted them? These are good questions, and they deserve answers. And like a good theologian and teacher of the faith, Paul faces them head-on. His answers have a profound bearing on all unbelievers and believers. So let's be sure to pay close attention.

FIRST, A MIND REFRESHER

Before we go any further, this is a good place to refresh our memories regarding what Paul has said to this point. So, as you reflect on what you've learned and possibly review the notes you've made in the previous lessons, summarize the main points of Romans 1—8 so you can see the overall case Paul has been building.

Now flip over to Romans 12 and read the first several verses. Does it seem as if Paul could have skipped chapters 9—11? Why or why not?

Why do you think he included these chapters? And why does his mood change from triumphant joy (Rom. 8) to "great sorrow and continual grief"? (9:2) Romans 9:3 holds the key.

NOW, A BIRD'S-EYE PERSPECTIVE

Now let's jump into Romans 9—11. We'll get started by gaining an overview of these chapters. Take some time to read them, and, as you do, see if you can find the answers to these questions:

Whom does Paul address in these chapters? Believers? Unbelievers? Gentiles? Jews?

What are the issues that concern Paul in relationship to these people?

What issues or questions do these chapters raise for you?

God's Faithful Blessings

Paul begins by naming some of the wonderful blessings the Jewish people have received from the hands of their faithful Lord (9:4, 5). What are these blessings?

Word Wealth

Israelites (v. 4): The descendants of Jacob, who had been renamed Israel (Gen. 32:28). Designations such as "Israel" and "Israelites" conveyed to Jews that they were God's chosen people.

Adoption (v. 4): This term refers to God's adoption of the nation of Israel as His son (Ex. 4:22, 23; Jer. 31:9; Hos. 11:1).

Glory (v. 4): The majestic manifestation of God's presence, which, during Israel's history, often occurred in the form of a radiant, almost blinding cloud (Ex. 16:7, 10; 40:34–38; Ezek. 1:28).

Covenants (v. 4): Pacts or treaties God made with individuals (such as Abraham, Gen. 15:1–21, and David, 2 Sam. 23:5) and the nation of Israel (Ex. 19:5; 24:1–8).

Law (v. 4): The set of instructions God gave the nation of Israel through Moses (Ex.).

Service (v. 4): The instructions God gave to Moses concerning Israel's worship of Him (Lev.; see also Heb. 9:1–6).

Promises (v. 4): The hundreds of promises God made to Israel throughout the Old Testament (see also Acts 13:29–39; Eph. 2:12).

Fathers (v. 5): Sometimes called *patriarchs*, these are Abraham, Isaac, Jacob, Jacob's twelve sons, and other notables in Israel's history, such as David (Mark 11:10; Acts 2:29).

Faith Alive

When was the last time you considered all the Lord has done for you? Take some time now to count your blessings and thank God for His loving, gracious gifts.

WHY UNBELIEF, THEN?

Since the Israelites have so much going for them, why have so many of them not trusted in Jesus as the long-awaited Messiah? Aren't all Israelites God's chosen and therefore saved no matter how they respond to Jesus? Paul's answer begins in 9:6–13 (see also 2:28, 29). Put it in your own words:

 BEHIND THE SCENES

The two Old Testament examples of God's choice revolve around Isaac and Ishmael, and Jacob and Esau. Neither example concerns the salvation of these individuals, but both involve God's making a choice among the physical descendants of Abraham for the establishment of the spiritual line of promise. Through whom would the Messiah come? Through Isaac's line or through Ishmael's? God declared that the Messiah would come through Isaac's line (Gen. 21:12). And what about the twins, Jacob and Esau? Once again, God made a sovereign choice, electing Jacob as the one through whom the messianic line would continue (Gen. 25:23).

When the text says that God loved Jacob but hated Esau, it does not mean that God cared for one and despised the other. Rather, the love-hate idea concerns God's choice of one twin over the other to carry on the physical line of the Messiah; it has nothing to do with His commitment to or feelings toward either person (see Matt. 6:24; Luke 14:26; John 12:25). God loves all human beings and desires only their best, if they will but choose Him by faith (John 3:16–18; 1 Tim. 2:3–6). Jacob and Esau, and Isaac and Ishmael all had the very real opportunity to freely accept or reject a faith-relationship with the Lord.

ABSOLUTELY A JUST JUDGE!

With God's willingness and sovereignty to choose firmly demonstrated from Israel's history, Paul considers the objection that such action on God's part leads to the conclusion that He is unjust (Rom. 9:14). Denying that, Paul appeals to the Old Testament story about Moses and Pharaoh and the Exodus of the Israelites from Egypt (vv. 15–18) to show that God has every right to show mercy to whomever He wants.

Do you remember the story? God's chosen people are enslaved in Egypt. He hears their cries for help and enlists Moses to act as His spokesman before Pharaoh, the ruler of Egypt. Before Moses goes in front of Pharaoh, however, God tells him that Pharaoh will not let the Israelites leave willingly. He says that He will harden Pharaoh's heart so that he will put up a fight and refuse to grant Moses' request to release the Israelites. Why would God do such a thing? Paul tells us by citing the words Moses spoke to Pharaoh: "For this very purpose I have raised you [Pharaoh] up, that I may show My power in you, and that My name may be declared in all the earth" (Rom. 9:17; cf. Ex. 9:16). The rest is history. Pharaoh might have been a gracious liberator, but he chose to be a hateful one. He did eventually release the Israelites, but not until some incredible miracles had occurred in Egypt—supernatural events that convinced both the Egyptians and the Israelites that the God of the Israelites was Lord over all.

But notice once again that the issue of personal salvation is not in view here. Paul is making a case for God's right to choose and that His choice is always just. So far, however, no one's salvation from everlasting death to everlasting life has been the focus in his examples.

   WORD WEALTH

Mercy (v. 15): Going beyond justice to give a person what is not deserved or to restrain from giving a person what is deserved; showing kindness and concern for someone in serious need.

Hardens (v. 18): Since this Greek word translated *hardens* refers to the Hebrew words used for *harden* in Exodus, we need to look back to the Hebrew terms to understand what Paul means.

The three Hebrew words translated *hardened* in the Exodus account of Pharaoh's hardening his heart have similar meanings. The word most frequently used means "to make strong, to strengthen, to harden" (Ex. 4:21; 7:13, 22; 8:19; 9:12, 35; 10:20, 27; 11:10; 14:4, 8, 17). The next most commonly used word (which is translated once as *stubborn*, Ex. 7:14) means "dullness" or "insensitivity" (Ex. 8:15, 32; 9:7, 34; 10:1). The third Hebrew term occurs once (Ex. 7:3), and it means "stubborn, stiff-necked."

When considered together and in their various contexts, none of these words carry the idea of someone's being forced to do something against his or her will. Instead, these terms convey the idea that Pharaoh was made more tenacious in his own already chosen path of pride and rebellion.

 FAITH ALIVE

Is your heart hard in any areas? Have you locked it away from God? If so, soften it toward Him today. Don't wait for His chastening hand to cast the deciding vote.

And if you know someone who has hardened herself toward the Lord, keep her in your prayers. She needs your prayerful intervention now more than ever.

YOU CAN'T BLAME ME . . . OR CAN YOU?

At this point Paul considers a very natural question but one built, in this case at least, on an attitude of arrogance and disbelief. If God makes the choices concerning to whom He shows mercy and whom He hardens, "Why does He still find fault? For who has resisted His will?" (Rom. 9:19). What is Paul's answer to this issue? (vv. 20–29) See if you can put it into your own words.

What would you say is the emphasis in Romans 9:1–29? Is greater stress placed on God's mercy or on His judgment? On His compassion or on His hardening activity? On His blessings or on His cursings? On His desire to spare people or on His desire to exercise His wrath against them?

Moreover, what is the focus of God's selecting activity in these verses? Is He seen choosing to condemn or choosing to bring blessing and understanding?

 FAITH ALIVE

What would you say is the significance of these emphases and focus for how God deals with you and those you know? How do you think these facts should change the way you respond to God and others?

Up to this point in Romans 9, Paul has clearly established that Israel is responsible for rejecting God's plan for them, and God is responsible for continually working with a rebellious people out of His infinite mercy and compassion. From here, Paul raises the question that every Jewish unbeliever would ask in light of the fact that Gentiles were attaining to a right standing before God while many Israelites were not (vv. 30, 31). Why was this so? Summarize Paul's answer (vv. 32, 33).

THE GOSPEL FOR ISRAEL

Romans 10:1–13 is Paul's gospel presentation to the Jewish people. You could call it "the Roman road of the plan of salvation for Israel." What is that plan? Is it any different from the gospel Paul preached to Gentiles?

Has Israel ever heard the gospel before? After all, how could they be held responsible for a message they never heard? "Ah," says Paul, "but they have heard, and they rejected it." How and when? Look at Paul's answer in 10:14–21 and see if you can restate it here.

Does this mean that God has turned His back on His chosen people? (11:1) "Certainly not!" exclaims Paul. What evidence does he cite in support of this negative response?

Paul himself (v. 1):

Elijah (vv. 2–4):

Conclusion (vv. 5, 6):

Why, then, have some accepted the gospel while others have not? (vv. 7–10)

Does this mean that those who have not yet accepted the gospel may never have an opportunity to do so? In fact, why would God seemingly make it so hard for unbelieving Jews to come to righteousness by faith? (vv. 11–32)

 WORD WEALTH

Blindness (v. 25): "Hardening, callousness. The word is a medical term describing the process by which extremities of fractured bones are set by an ossifying, or calloused petrifying. Sometimes it describes a hard substance in the eye that blinds. Used metaphorically, [it] denotes a dulled spiritual perceptivity, spiritual blindness, and hardness."[1] Notice in 11:25 that this blindness is partial (because throughout this time a remnant is saved), and it is temporary (because it will end when "the fullness of the Gentiles has come in").

How should Gentiles feel about all this? What should be their response personally, publicly, and pastorally? (vv. 11–32)

How long will this state of blindness last for Israel? (v. 25)

What does "the fullness of the Gentiles" (v. 25) mean, and how does it relate to the "fullness" of the Jews? (v. 12) Some related passages are Luke 21:24; John 10:16; Acts 15:14.

When Paul says "all Israel will be saved" (v. 26) after the fullness of the Gentiles has come, what does he mean? Bible commentators generally hold one of three views regarding this passage's interpretation. Reflect on each option in light of what you have learned in Romans so far and see which view you think has the greatest biblical support.

Option 1: "All Israel" refers to the total number of Jews and Gentiles in every generation who come to salvation by faith.

Option 2: "All Israel" designates all the Jews of every generation who come to salvation by faith.

Option 3: "All Israel" denotes the great number of Jews in the final generation who will come to salvation by faith.

Can you see how these three ideas might be conveyed?

FAITH ALIVE

Paul's attitude toward the needs of the Jews for salvation is more than commendable—it's godly. Do you know any Jewish people who need the Savior? Whether you do or not, would you be willing to pray consistently for their salvation? The Lord has not given up on His chosen people; He has not forgotten His promises for them. Neither should we.

A GLANCE BACK

Review what we have covered in this lesson and see if you can summarize the main argument of Romans 9:1—11:32. When all is said and done, what is Paul driving at in this portion of Scripture and what are his major supporting points?

A FITTING CLOSE

In the final four verses of Romans 11, Paul launches into a doxology—a fitting way to end some of the most incredible truths regarding God's ways in human history. In this outburst of praise, how does Paul describe God? List as many characteristics as you can.

PROBING THE DEPTHS

Turn your eyes heavenward, thinking about what Paul has said about God in these final verses, and just praise Him for who He is and what He has done. Worthy is the Lord, worthy to be praised. Alleluia!

Fewer topics create more heat than light than the subject of the relationship between divine sovereignty and human freedom. Some people emphasize God's sovereignty to the exclusion of human freedom. Others downplay God's sovereignty and exalt human freedom. Many people just throw up their hands, claiming that the issue is absolutely impossible to resolve because it contradicts reason.

If you would like to dig deeper into this whole discussion, I have listed some books below that will help you wade through the labyrinth while presenting a number of different positions.

Basinger, David, and Randall Basinger. *Predestination and Free Will: Four Views of Divine Sovereignty and Human Freedom.* Downers Grove, IL: InterVarsity Press, 1986.

Billheimer, Paul E. *The Mystery of God's Providence.* Wheaton, IL: Tyndale House, 1983.

Craig, William Lane. *The Only Wise God: The Compatibility of Divine Foreknowledge and Human Freedom.* Grand Rapids, MI: Baker Book House, 1987.

Fisk, Samuel. *Divine Sovereignty and Human Freedom.* Neptune, NJ: Loizeaux Brothers, 1973.

Forster, Roger T., and V. Paul Marston. *God's Strategy in Human History.* Wheaton, IL: Tyndale House, 1973.

Packer, J. I. *Evangelism and the Sovereignty of God.* Downers Grove, IL: InterVarsity Press, 1961.

Pinnock, Clark H., ed. *The Grace of God, the Will of Man.* Grand Rapids, MI: Zondervan Publishing House, 1989.

_____. *Grace Unlimited.* Minneapolis, MN: Bethany Fellowship, 1975.

Rupp, E. Gordon, and Philip S. Watson, eds. *Luther and Erasmus: Free Will and Salvation.* Philadelphia, PA: Westminster Press, 1969.

Shank, Robert. *Elect in the Son.* Minneapolis, MN: Bethany House, 1989.

---

1. *Spirit-Filled Life Bible* (Nashville, TN: Thomas Nelson Publishers, 1991), 1706, "Word Wealth: 11:25 blindness."

Lesson 10/Transformed Sacrifices (12:1–21)

- Look out for number one.
- Life is short, so grab all the gusto you can.
- You can have it all in the here and now.
- Don't be a mat for anyone.
- If someone knocks you down, get up and hit him harder.
- Winning is everything.
- People only remember those who come in first, so don't settle for second.

I could continue the list, but you get the picture. You see it everyday—through television, movies, sports events, newspapers, countless books, friends, and family. Getting what you want, when you want it, as often as you want it, and however you want it is our society's message. It's what we're supposed to go after, to model. It's presented as the key to living happily ever after. But is it true? Can it really deliver what it promises?

The Bible says no. Serving self first will never bring lasting happiness. Sure, it may feel good for the short haul. In fact, you may even feel as if you deserve to have your needs and wants met above those of others. But if you really live with self-service as your maxim, you will miss genuine, lasting joy. You will miss the Christian life and all the blessings that come with it because the life we are to live through Christ begins with other-service, which is just another name for self-sacrifice.

But don't misunderstand me. This is not the kind of sacrifice where you flagellate yourself until others feel better or get what they want. No. This is transformed sacrificial living. It changes our character, our minds, our hearts, until our most basic drive in life is to help others, to serve them in every way we can so they too will not only see but desire and even begin to live and enjoy the life of other-centered living in Christ.

"How can this be? It seems so backward, so contrary to the way our society wants us to live." That's just the point. God's perspective is right-side up, while ours is really upside down. We think our viewpoint is normal, but it isn't. Our perspective is messed up, confused, irrational. God's is perfect, clear, and eminently rational. So if you have to, work through this lesson standing on your head—intellectually and practically, that is. Paul is about to reorient our thinking so it resembles God's.

THE KEY TO THE CHRISTIAN LIFE

The first eleven chapters of Romans, though marked with life applications, are largely doctrinal. Paul lays the theological foundation and scope of the gospel, and defends it against misunderstandings and objections. But once he reaches chapter 12, his focus changes dramatically. "I beseech you therefore, brethren" are words that look back and build on all the groundwork Paul has laid. "With all that in mind," Paul says, "I plead with you, fellow believers, to . . ." What? What does he want us to do in light of the gospel message? It begins and is summed up in the first three verses of chapter 12. Try to restate those verses in your own words.

v. 1

v. 2

v. 3

Let's look at these verses more closely. They contain four commands, and each one is linked to each of the others, forming a bond that ties together all the other practical counsel that follows in Romans. These four directives are the keys to the Christian life. They unlock the gospel's practical power in the lives of those saved by our Lord Jesus Christ and indwelt by the Holy Spirit.

What phrase does Paul use to sum up God's activity in the giving and outworking of the gospel of Jesus Christ? (v. 1)

Paul's first command involves doing something with our bodies. But the word he uses for bodies doesn't mean just our physical body. The word *bodies* is a metaphor standing for all that we are—be it physical or spiritual, emotional or mental. So what does it mean to offer our whole selves to God as "a living sacrifice"? (v. 1) What implications are here concerning our worship practices?

Is our sacrificial offering to be a once-for-all act or an occasional act or a frequent one or even a daily one? How do you know?

In verse 1, what four descriptions tell us about the type of sacrifice we are to make?

What do these descriptions tell us about God's nature and character and expectations?

After calling us to be consecrated, Paul tells us to "not be conformed to this world" (v. 2). The Bible talks about "the world" and its pitfalls in several places. Look up the following passages and summarize what they say about the world's condition and allurements and how we should relate to them, especially in light of Paul's command in Romans 12:2.

Matt. 13:22

Gal. 1:4

1 Pet. 1:14

1 John 2:15–17

Paul's next command is positive, and it is set in contrast to his nonconformity command. Whereas *conformed* has to do with shaping ourselves according to an outward appearance or pattern, *transformed* refers to inner changes that lead to outward expressions of those inner changes. How does this transformation take place? (Rom. 12:2)

What is the goal of the transformation process? (v. 2)

The fourth command Paul gives is found in verse 3, and it has two sides to it—a negative and a positive. What are they?

The negative:

The positive:

 FAITH ALIVE

Before we press on, go back through these four keys to the Christian life and consider their role in *your* life. Are you actively obeying them? If not, what steps can you begin taking this week to obey them in very down-to-earth ways? Be specific.

Be Consecrated

Don't Be Conformed

Be Transformed

Maintain a Proper Self-Perspective

GIFTS OF SERVICE

Consecration, nonconformity, transformation, evaluation—these are all acts of individuals looking inward, assessing and redirecting themselves in the power of God's Spirit toward a godly character, perspective, and life-style. Once we are actively engaged there, however, we will have to move outward, toward serving others. The Christian life was never meant to be lived apart from community. We are not loners for Christ—rugged individualists looking out only for ourselves. Any self-directed work must eventually turn to other-directed work. Just as Christ came to save and serve others, so He calls on us, His adopted children, to reach out to others with His salvation message and to help them grow up in the family of faith.

Now God doesn't just call us to service and then leave us on our own. He never leaves us in the lurch. Whatever He calls us to do, He also equips us to do. As Paul says, "God has dealt to each one a measure of faith" (v. 3). The "faith" here is "not saving faith but the faith to receive and to exercise the gifts God apportions to us."[1] God gives us the gifts and the faith we need to use those gifts. Realizing this, let's turn our attention to verses 4–8.

Before Paul mentions any of the gifts by name, he talks about the church, the body of Christ. What does he say about it? (vv. 4, 5)

What is the significance of this description of the church? You may also want to consult two parallel passages: 1 Corinthians 12:4–27 and Ephesians 4:11–16.

In Romans 12:6–8, seven gifts are mentioned. What are they, and how is each to be used?

SPIRITUAL GIFTS OF SERVICE

THE GIFTS	HOW TO USE THEM
1)	
2)	
3)	
4)	
5)	
6)	
7)	

WORD WEALTH

Basically, two interpretations are taken on this passage concerning gifts. One is that this list of gifts indicates creational gifts—"inherent tendencies that characterize each different person by reason of the Creator's unique workmanship in their initial gifting."[2] When viewed in this light, this gift-listing is different from the lists given elsewhere in the New Testament. The gifts mentioned in Romans flow from the Father and form our "foundational motivation in life and service to God," while the gift-listing in Ephesians 4 flows from the Son and describes church offices, and the gift-listing in 1 Corinthians 12 flows from the Spirit and describes empowered abilities given to us "for edifying the church and evangelizing the world."[3]

The second interpretation views the gifts mentioned in Romans "as a repeat or overlap of many of those mentioned in either 1 Cor. 12:12–29 or Eph. 4:11."[4]

I will represent both positions in the following definitions, giving the creation-gift interpretation first.

Prophesy (v. 6): Either (1) the ability "to view all of life with special ongoing prophetic insight, independent of public office or special use by the Spirit in giving public prophecy," or (2) "the manifestation of public prophecy, speaking something that God has spontaneously brought to mind (1 Cor. 12:10)."[5]

Ministry (v. 7): Either (1) the ability "to most effectively serve the body [of Christ] in physical ways," or (2) "the rendering of any type of service by anyone in the church."[6]

Teaches (v. 7): Either (1) the gift "to keep an eye on and instruct the revealed truth of God's Word, regardless of public office," or (2) "the public office of teacher (Eph. 4:11)."[7]

Exhorts (v. 8): Either (1) the ability "to best apply God's truths through encouragement," or (2) "those (such as pastors) who are called to publicly bring encouragement to the church."[8]

Gives (v. 8): Either (1) "those gifted to contribute to the emotional and/or physical support of others," or (2) "those gifted with abundant financial means so as to support the work of the gospel."[9]

Leads (v. 8): Either (1) the giftedness "to effectively facilitate all areas of life," or (2) "the public function of administration (1 Cor. 12:28)."[10]

Mercy (v. 8): Either (1) "the special gift of strong, perceptive emotions," or (2) "special functions of Christian relief or acts of charity."[11]

 ## FAITH ALIVE

Regardless of which gift or mixture of gifts you have been given, how are you using what you have? Are you using your giftedness as God desires, or are you misusing it for your own gain? Consider this issue carefully, asking God to unveil the secret matters of the heart so you can truly be His faithful servant for His church.

THE EXHORTATIONS OF LOVE

At the heart of transformed sacrificial living is love. In fact, without love, that kind of living is impossible. Although the word *love* does not appear throughout verses 9–21, love is definitely the guiding principle (v. 9), the beacon that illuminates and directs our personal lives (vv. 9, 11, 12) as well as our relationships with fellow Christians and with our adversaries (vv. 10, 13–21).

Paul speaks of three characteristics of love in verse 9. What are they?

 FAITH ALIVE

Review each of love's characteristics, then examine yourself in light of each. Is your love sincere and consistent? Does your love recoil in the face of evil and revel in the face of good? Are you compromising your love in any way, say by flirting with what you know is wrong or by failing to stand up for what is right? Be transparent before the Lord. Allow Him to redirect any of your mistaken steps and purify your love for His name's sake.

Verses 9–21 give us twenty exhortations. Restate each one in your own words, then pick out the ones that are the most difficult for you to obey and write down one or two things you can do with God's enabling grace to make them a part of your transformed life-style.

LOVE'S EXHORTATIONS	MY COMMITMENTS
1.	
2.	
3.	
4.	

5.

6.

7.

8.

9.

10.

11.

12.

13.

14.

15.

16.

17.

18.

19.

20.

 BEHIND THE SCENES

Verse 20 requires some explanation. At first blush, the verse appears to present a backhanded way we can get revenge against our enemies. All we have to do, the verse seems to say, is be especially nice to them, and in turn our actions will increase the level of the condemnation our enemies will experience at the hands of God. If verse 20 really taught this, it would contradict the spirit of the verse's entire context. Rather, providing an opportunity for our enemies to repent and find forgiveness is what this verse is conveying. In other words, by returning evil with good, evil can be conquered rather than perpetuated by acts of vengeance. After all, what better way to conquer evil than by loving evildoers so much that they turn from evil and commit themselves to good? Isn't that what God the Father is seeking to do through His supreme act of sacrifice and love—the giving of His Son on our behalf, even to the point of crucifixion?

Transformed living. To the world, its practitioners seem like beings from another planet. Who in their right mind would repay evil committed against them with good or serve others more than themselves or pass up the world's allurements for some intangible joys? It doesn't make sense! Right? Wrong. It makes perfect sense. Once we remember that this world is fallen, so it cannot stand as the rule for what's right and reasonable, and once we recall that only God is the perfect, unchanging standard for what's good and rational, then those who follow His way are the ones to look to for what makes sense.

Which way are you following? The world's or God's? Following the crowd, conforming yourself to what everyone else is doing is easy. But it's also destructive. God has a much better, more sane track to follow. Yes, it's harder, but He will always give you what you need to live life His way.

Transformed living. That's what I want. How about you?

1. *Spirit-Filled Life Bible* (Nashville, TN: Thomas Nelson Publishers, 1991), 1708, note on 12:3.
2. Ibid., 2022–2023.
3. Ibid., 2023.
4. Ibid., 1708, note on 12:6–8.
5. Ibid., note on 12:6.
6. Ibid., note on 12:7, 8.
7. Ibid.
8. Ibid.
9. Ibid.
10. Ibid.
11. Ibid.

Lesson 11/Citizenship for Pilgrims (13:1–14)

The Bible refuses to let us forget that our home is not here. We are pilgrims, foreigners in an alien land. Our true home, the one we are looking forward to entering, is heaven. And it is there, says Paul, that our citizenship lies (Phil. 3:20).

But therein lies the rub. We are not actually in heaven right now; we're on earth. And here we have homes, mortgages, pay taxes, vote, attend church, worship, work, play, and go about life as citizens of earthly countries. In truth, we have dual citizenships, and that means we have dual loyalties. Like it or not, we have commitments here on earth, not just in heaven. We have authorities other than God to answer to, and that creates conflict, especially when those earthly authorities—knowingly or unknowingly—go against God's revealed values and command us to as well. History is replete with such examples. Governments have sanctioned slavery, abortion, idolatry, homosexuality, divorce for virtually any reason, stealing, lying, murder, greed, genocide, and ecological destruction. What are Christians to do in such circumstances? Which loyalties should win out? Whom should we obey?

Romans 13 is one of the key biblical passages that deals with this issue. Here we'll learn some of what citizenship for pilgrims involves—its benefits and costs, its securities and dangers, its problems and solutions.

THE FOUNDATION FOR GOOD CITIZENSHIP

The foundational principle for our earthly citizenship is revealed in verse 1. Take a moment to recopy it here:

Who is to submit to civil government?

Where do earthly governmental authorities get their ultimate authority to rule?

According to this verse, are there any governing authorities that derive their ultimate authority to rule from any other source than God?

Without looking ahead in Romans 13, what are the implications you see that flow from verse 1?

What questions do these implications raise in your own mind?

How do you relate 1 Timothy 2:1–3 to this passage?

THE PRICE OF DISOBEDIENCE

Since God is the supreme authority, why not ignore or even disobey the established laws of civil government on the pretext that we are obeying a higher power, a greater authority? Paul gives us four reasons to be good, law-abiding citizens rather than resisters of the state.

Reason 1 (v. 2):

Reason 2 (v. 2):

Reason 3 (vv. 3, 4):

Reason 4 (v. 5):

PAYMENT DUE

So how should we then live as pilgrims with earthly citizenship? Paul sums up his answer in verses 6, 7. See if you can capsulize it in your own words.

 WORD WEALTH

Taxes (vv. 6, 7): Monetary obligations due to the state for personal property.

Customs (v. 7): Monies due for importing and exporting goods.

Fear (v. 7): Reverence or respect.

Honor (v. 7): Allegiance or loyalty.

 FAITH ALIVE

Though few like to pay taxes and customs duties, the biblical admonition is clear—we must pay to the state what is due. Are you faithful in that regard?

Moreover, the Bible is also clear that civil authorities should receive our respect and loyalty, not just our financial obligations. Do those traits mark your earthly citizenship?

Ponder these areas of your life in light of Romans 13. Consider what may call for your repentance and think about what changes you should make. Record your thoughts below.

BIBLE EXTRA

Romans 13:1–7 raises some important questions that Christians have wrestled with for centuries. Without taking sides on these matters, I have listed many of these questions and occasionally cited some other biblical texts that may help you in your thinking. Approach these matters as objectively as you can, allowing the Scriptures to speak for themselves.

Should Christians try to alter government policies and laws so they conform to biblical standards, or should they support laws that allow people to live and believe contrary to the Bible? (Consider Christians in lands where no freedom, no voting voice, no public gatherings are allowed. How ought they to live in the face of unbiblical government policies?)

Is state-supported capital punishment right or wrong? See also Genesis 9:6; Exodus 20:13; 21:12–17, 23–25; 22:18–20; Leviticus 20:1–21; John 8:1–12.

Does Romans 13 support, oppose, or remain neutral on the issue of the separation of church and state? Can you think of other passages that may help resolve this issue?

Is it always wrong to resist the laws of the land? If not, under what condition(s) may disobedience to the state be justified? See Exodus 1:8–21; 2:11–15; Daniel 3 and 6; Mark 12:13–17; Acts 4:1–31; 5:12–42; 16:35–40; Titus 3:1; 1 Peter 2:13–17.

If civil disobedience is permissible, is it ever right to strive to avoid the state's punishment for violating its laws? You may want to reconsult the passages listed with the previous question.

What forms of civil disobedience, if permissible, would be allowable? Peaceable protests? Picketing? Refusal to pay taxes? Armed resistance? Treason? Deceit? As you think about this, keep in mind some real historical conflicts, such as the American Revolution, the Civil War, the attempted rescue attempts of persecuted Jews under Hitler's regime, the demonstrations of pro-life groups against abortion clinics. Based on your understanding of Scripture, what would be a Christian response in the midst of such conflicts?

Does the Bible support one type of government (democratic, monarchial, socialist) over another? Does the type of government a Christian is under impact at all what Paul says in Romans 13? Support your answers from Scripture as much as possible.

THE TIME-HONORED DEBT OF LOVE

Paul now turns from our relationship to civil governing authorities to our interpersonal relationships in and outside the body of Christ.

What one characteristic should permeate all our relationships? (v. 8)

What is Paul's biblical case for this claim? (vv. 8–10) Summarize his argument.

FAITH ALIVE

Can you say that love is the hallmark of all your interpersonal relationships? Is it the only nonfinancial debt you seek to repay anyone? Or do you sometimes repay with hurt, dishonesty, disloyalty, snobbery, or other unloving actions?

Let's take an inventory. Use the chart below to help you assess your relationships against the standard of unconditional love. Check "High" if your relationship is almost always very loving, "Medium" if it's usually loving, "Low" if love still exists but is very strained and rarely expressed, and "Missing in Action" if love can't be found. How are you doing?

MY RELATIONSHIPS	MY LEVEL OF LOVING			
	High	Medium	Low	Missing in Action
Spouse				
Children				
Mother				
Father				
Friends				
Work Associates				
Church Family				
Neighbors				
Strangers				

Now reflect on your answers and think of one step you can take this week to improve the level of love in each of those relationships that scored in the "Low" or "Missing in Action" categories.

SOUND THE ALARM!

Paul ends Romans 13 with a wake-up call. Now is not the time to be lazy or complacent—to live as if we are on a sinking ship that demands or needs nothing from us. In spite of the darkness of sin that surrounds us, Paul challenges us to live in a certain way. Read verses 11–14; then answer the following questions.

What should we strip from our lives?

What should we clothe ourselves with?

Why should we heed Paul's call?

When Paul says that "our salvation *is* nearer than when we *first* believed" and "the day is at hand," what does he mean? What is he referring to? See also Mark 13:28–37; Romans 8:22, 23; Hebrews 9:28; James 5:7–9; 1 Peter 1:3–9.

 FAITH ALIVE

Paul has sounded the alarm. Have you heard it? Are you living with the expectation of Christ's return? Will He be pleased with your life commitment to Him? Will He find you wrapped in Himself or covered with yourself? Journal your thoughts below. Make them a prayer of confession, petition, and praise to God. Then expect Him to answer. He always responds to the humble of heart.

Lesson 12/Liberating Love
(14:1—15:13)

If you ever want to put a spark in a gathering of Christians, voice a position about drinking alcoholic beverages, or gambling, or smoking, or celebrating Halloween, or listening to rock music, or dancing, or attending R-rated movies, or whether you can be a Democrat or a Republican and still be a Christian. If you like, you could move beyond these social issues to more theological ones, such as whether Jesus' return will come before, simultaneously with, or after the Rapture, or whether there will even be a Rapture, or whether foot-washing should be treated as a sacrament, or whether new believers should be baptized by immersion, pouring, or sprinkling, or which musical instruments are permissible to use in a worship service, or whether women can be deacons or elders or preachers. Raise any of these issues—or any number of others—and watch what happens. The conversation may start politely enough, but soon you'll find signs of deep-seated disagreements, sometimes even hostility. Can't you hear the comments?

- You don't really believe that, do you?
- At First Church of _____ [you fill in the blank] we would never permit that!
- I knew someone who believed that, but they also got divorced and one of their kids ended up on drugs. That's what happens when you go liberal.
- Hell is filled with people who think as you do!
- You can think that if you want—it's a free country. Oh, by the way, have you ever accepted Jesus as your Savior?
- You should set up an appointment with my pastor. He will set you straight on this matter. He has Bible verses for everything.

With as much as Christians agree upon, it's absolutely amazing to see what we can fight about, even split churches over. This habit is nothing new, unfortunately. It has been with the church since its inception. And in those early days, God gave His people a way to handle these matters so they wouldn't become divisive. His plan? *Liberating love.* And it's spelled out in Romans 14:1—15:13, which describes two groups who are at odds with each other over two areas of concern. So let's keep open minds, laying aside our differences so we can hear what He has to say to us. We have nothing to lose, except, of course, petty squabbling, infighting, prejudice, intolerance, and the world's opinion that we have nothing of value to offer.

THE FACTIONS, THE ISSUES, THE CONSEQUENCES

We'll begin with an overview. Read Romans 14:1—15:13; then answer the following questions.

What are the two factions?

What are the two disputing issues?

Does Paul consider both groups Christian? Support your answer.

What were these groups doing to each other? (14:3, 10, 13, 15, 16, 21)

What impact was their dispute having on God's work? (14:20)

Overall, what is Paul's advice to these warring factions?

 BEHIND THE SCENES

You probably noticed that Paul doesn't provide very many details about the nature of this dispute in the first-century Christian community of Rome. From the text, we know that it concerned heartfelt differences of opinion over special diets and special days (14:3, 5), but beyond that the information is very sketchy. It could be that because the Roman church was comprised of Gentiles and Jews, they were fighting over whether to maintain the Jewish holy days and dietary laws. Or maybe some individuals had no problem eating meat sacrificed to idols and treating Saturday—the Jewish Sabbath day—as just another day of the week, while others were adamant that food used in idol worship was taboo and the traditional Sabbath still should be observed as a special day of worship and rest.[1] Whatever the specifics, one thing is clear: the groups were dividing over nonessentials— matters that were not critical to Christian belief or practice— and their disputing was causing injury to the body and cause of Christ. That was important enough for the Spirit of God to inspire Paul's words of rebuke, correction, and exhortation.

GUIDELINES FOR PRESERVING UNITY

Paul gives very practical, timeless counsel on how believers can get along with one another even when they hold differences of opinion over important yet nonessential beliefs and practices.

Why should we avoid judging other believers over "doubtful things" (14:1)—beliefs and practices neither required nor forbidden in Scripture?

14:3

14:4

14:7–12

Is any created thing really taboo? (v. 14; cf. 1 Cor. 10:25, 26; Titus 1:15)

How should stronger Christians deal with their weaker brethren who believe some things are forbidden even when they are not?

14:21

15:1, 2

Why should the stronger believers treat the weaker ones this way?

14:15

14:17–19

14:20

15:3

By behaving this way, are the stronger Christians capitulating to the mistaken beliefs of weaker Christians, even placing their stamp of approval on those beliefs? Explain your answer.

When we aren't sure if something is right or wrong, what should we do? (14:22, 23)

PRESERVE THE UNION!

The bottom line in all of this is the preservation of unity among the household of faith. Paul emphasizes, illustrates, and supports this point in 15:5–12, then wraps it up with a prayer in verse 13. Let's look at what he says more closely.

Unity means "like-mindedness" (v. 5). Does this mean that Christians should believe and do the same things in everything? Why or why not? Do your best to support your answer from Romans 14 and 15.

What is God's role in the unifying process? (v. 5)

What is our role? (v. 7)

What role has Jesus played in laying the foundation for Christian unity? (vv. 8–12)

What qualities of God does Paul mention? (v. 5) Why do you think he singles these out?

What is the ultimate goal of unity? (v. 6)

What makes the prayer in verse 13 an apt ending to this whole discussion on divisiveness and unity in the body of Christ?

 ### FAITH ALIVE

Before moving on, ask the Lord to help you become more mature in the faith in those areas where you still may be weak. Also ask Him to show you when and how you should support weaker brothers and sisters in the faith out of liberating love. Both of these requests are within His will, so He will certainly answer you.

---

1. If you would like to consult some sources on the exact nature of the disputes in view here, see commentaries cited in earlier endnotes.

Lesson 13/On the Road Again (15:14–33)

If you're a human being, you've likely made at least one trip in your lifetime. Maybe it was to a nearby town or to another end of your state. Or maybe you went on a longer journey, crossing several state lines or perhaps even traveling outside of the U.S. You may have hit the road in a car, a bus, a train, or bypassed all the experiences of land travel and gone by water or air. Wherever or however you went, the trip was likely memorable, and it was definitely more comfortable than traveling during New Testament times.

Imagine you're in the Mediterranean region during the first century. Although you occasionally have access to some of the wider, better constructed and nicely paved Roman roads, most of your land travel is on roads that are like those made by the American pioneers when they first traveled westward across mountains and plains. Even modern jeeps would have trouble traveling many of these roadways. So, for the most part, you have to walk.

Now suppose you decide to plan a long trip, beginning in Jerusalem, going northwest through modern-day Turkey and into modern-day Greece, to Athens and Corinth. Then from there, you want to take a ship east across the southern edge of the Aegean Sea to Ephesus, then continue your trip by sea, traveling southeast to Caesarea, the first-century capital of Palestine, then by land again to Jerusalem. The round-trip mileage is about 2,800 miles. What should you plan for?

First of all, you need to prepare for a very slow, long trip. In a carriage or wagon, which you'll be able to use only once in awhile, you'll be able to cover about 25 miles a day, and that's if you're on a very good Roman road. On foot, which is how you will likely travel most of the time, you'll be able to cover about 15 miles daily. If you can get access to a donkey, you'll increase your distance traveled to 20 miles daily. If you're really fortunate and can use a dromedary—a camel of unusual speed specially bred and trained for riding—you will move much faster, at about 70 miles a day, but you'll have to abandon him when you hit tough, mountainous terrain. Sea travel will be much better, allowing you to do around 55 nautical miles a day, but you won't take advantage of that until the last leg of your trip. Moreover, you'll have to make sure that your sea travel takes place between the end of May and the middle of September. You won't be able to get travel insurance during any other time of the sea-traveling year because of the severe winter storms that make such trips extremely hazardous.

Second, you will need to prepare for con artists and bandits of just about every variety. They can recognize a tourist almost immediately, and they show no mercy.

Third, because there are so few travel inns, you'd better have a lot of family, friends, and friends of friends scattered along your planned travel route so you will have a hot meal and a roof over your head at least sometimes.

Finally, you should plan for all kinds of weather. Given all the different types of terrain and climates you will encounter over your months of travel, you can expect to be in searing heat, bitter cold, and almost everything else in between.[1]

Sound like a treat? Those are just a few of the considerations the apostle Paul had to make during his missionary journeys. In fact, the round trip from Jerusalem to Corinth you just planned was the route Paul took on his second missionary journey. It was certainly no picnic.

As Paul comes to the end of his long letter to the believers in Rome, he tells them about his upcoming travel plans, including when he wants to come see them. Despite the hardships of travel, Paul is ready to hit the road again, but he wants the Roman Christians to know why, to understand what God has accomplished through him, and to solicit their support. What he says in these few verses speaks volumes to us—to our motivations, our ministries, our willingness to sacrifice, our values—if we're only willing to listen.

REWARDING WORDS

Throughout Romans, Paul has laid out the content of the gospel message, answered objections to it, corrected misinterpretations, and applied it. If he had said nothing else, his original readership—and all later readers—would have likely assumed that he covered this ground because he thought the Roman Christians didn't understand the gospel well enough to explain it and defend it, especially to those who threatened to undermine it through legalism or licentiousness. But in 15:14, Paul lays this assumption to rest. He expresses his confidence in these first-century believers through mentioning three truths about them. What are they?

WORD WEALTH

Goodness (v. 14): "Beneficence, kindness in actual manifestation, virtue equipped for action, a bountiful propensity both to will and to do what is good, intrinsic goodness producing a generosity and a [godly] state or being."[2]

Filled with all knowledge (v. 14): A comprehensive understanding of what is expected of believers.[3]

Admonish (v. 14): Counsel or warn. (The objective is to gain your hearer through graciousness, not alienate him or her through self-righteousness.)

FAITH ALIVE

Which of these characteristics could be ascribed to you? On a scale of 1 to 5, with 1 indicating only minor traces of these characteristics and 5 indicating their consistent presence in your life, how would you rate yourself?

	1	2	3	4	5
Goodness					
Knowledge					
Admonishing Ability					

What are some steps you can take to begin to move your rating closer to the 5 level? Don't ignore what you need God to help you accomplish.

With such high praise for these believers, why did Paul write them so extensively about the gospel? (vv. 15, 16)

 FAITH ALIVE

Think back on what we have covered in our Romans study. What did you already know about the gospel that we covered here? How was this reminder helpful to you? In other words, what are some of the truths that were driven home to you with new, life-changing force? Record your thoughts in this chart.

TRUTHS RECALLED	APPLICATIONS RENEWED

Did you notice in verse 16 that Paul had no trouble articulating his ministry focus? He knew what God had called him to do. Do you? If so, state it here as a reminder and affirmation of your calling. If you don't know what ministry God has for you, go to Him in prayer and ask Him to cause the Holy Spirit to reveal it to you. Make sure you really want to know and remain open to what He has in store for you.

WHEN SUCCESS BREEDS HUMILITY

Paul has probably been the greatest missionary in church history. And while he knew he had accomplished a lot, he was careful to say to whom the credit was due. Even as he rode on the crest of his success, humility never left his side.

To whom does Paul give credit for his evangelistic efforts, and what indications does he have that this Person was working through him? (vv. 17–19)

WORD WEALTH

Signs and wonders (v. 19): "Served to accredit the messenger of God and validate the message he brought" (Acts 2:22; 5:12; 2 Cor. 12:12).

Illyricum (v. 19): A Roman province northwest of Macedonia, and probably the closest Paul had gotten, up to this point in his travels, to Rome, Italy.[4]

FAITH ALIVE

How do you handle success? When you know God has worked through you, when you see evidence of His presence and power, do you give Him the credit or try to share the limelight or try to steal the show?

How can you boast in God rather than in yourself?

Why did Paul choose to preach the gospel to those who had not heard about Jesus Christ before? (vv. 20, 21)

Because Paul decided to go where no one had gone before to preach the gospel, does that mean that all our evangelistic efforts should be directed the same way? Should we only go to countries, cities, tribes, and so on, that have never heard the gospel? If not, why?

 FAITH ALIVE

Not everyone is called to do what Paul did, but all of us are called to play some part in spreading the good news of salvation in Jesus Christ (Matt. 28:18–20). What part are you playing?

If you aren't committed to any kind of evangelistic effort at this time, what would it take for you to become involved?

Ask the Lord to clear away any obstacles that are blocking you from reaching out to others with the gospel. He will be delighted to oblige.

THE ROUNDABOUT WAY TO SPAIN

In the final verses of Romans 15, Paul lays out his travel plans. But these verses do not contain just a simple itinerary. They go far beyond that, showing us the compassion, dedication, interdependence, fears, and heartfelt desires of a man of God.

Why had Paul been held back in his desire to go to Rome? (v. 22; cf. v. 20)

Given why Paul had not yet traveled to Rome, why do you think he planned to go to Spain? (vv. 24, 28)

Why did Paul say he wanted to spend time in Rome on his way further west? (vv. 24, 32; cf. 1:15)

As much as Paul wanted to go to Rome and Spain, even though he was already fairly close to these destinations, he said that he would first travel in the opposite direction and go to

Jerusalem. Why did he want to go so far out of his way? What did he want to do there and what made it so important? (15:25–28)

Paul was definitely committed to going to Jerusalem, but he also feared going there. Why? (vv. 30, 31)

BIBLE EXTRA

Other New Testament passages show that Paul's fears were certainly justified. In fact, he had had past problems with unbelieving religious Jews and certain other groups in the early church, and these groups would resurface when he returned to Jerusalem, and they would get him in trouble and sent to Rome in a way he had never expected to go. By reading the following passages, you will be able to retrace what happened to Paul and see how God used these events to spread the good news about His Son.
• The trouble Paul experienced from these groups prior to writing Romans and before leaving Corinth: Acts 9:20–30; 13:42–51; 14:1–6, 19, 20; 15:1–29; 17:1–15; 18:1–17.
• What Paul faced from these groups after leaving Corinth and writing Romans and how it led to his trip to Rome as a prisoner: Acts 19:1–20; 20:1–3, 17–37; 21:3—28:31.

BEHIND THE SCENES

We know from the final chapters of Acts that Paul made it from Jerusalem to Rome—as a prisoner of the Roman Empire. But did he ever make it to Spain? Bible scholars disagree. Some think that Paul was executed about two or so years after his recorded imprisonment in Acts. Other scholars believe that sometime after his imprisonment in Rome, he was freed, then traveled to Spain and preached the gospel as he had desired, then later ended up in Rome again as a prisoner and was executed there. The primary evidence they give for this conclusion comes from a letter written by a first-century Roman Christian named Clement.

A BLESSING

Paul knew that trouble awaited him in Jerusalem, but he would not be held back by that, neither would he let that dread sour his ministry. He wished the best for those he served, so he closed Romans 15 with a blessing: "Now the God of peace *be* with you all. Amen" (v. 33). It takes courage and character to face adversity that way, and the only One who can prepare us to do that is our heavenly Father working through His Son and Spirit.

If you're traveling down some tough roads now, or you know that just over the ridge trouble is waiting to ambush you, don't try to tackle it alone. Invite the God of peace to come alongside you as your travel companion. He may not deliver you from trouble's hands, but He will strengthen you to face adversity with Christ-like character and Spirit-directed power. Like Paul, you will be able to carry on, even in spite of any harm others may want to inflict on you.

So go with Him, and may He give you peace through whatever lies ahead.

1. See "Travel," by J. Kelso, in *The Zondervan Pictorial Encyclopedia of the Bible* (Grand Rapids, MI: Zondervan Publishing House, 1976), 5:799–807; Barry J. Beitzel, *The Moody Atlas of Bible Lands* (Chicago, IL: Moody Press, 1985), 176–185.

2. *Spirit-Filled Life Bible* (Nashville, TN: Thomas Nelson Publishers, 1991), 1713, "Word Wealth: 15:14 goodness."

3. Everett F. Harrison, "Romans," in *The Expositor's Bible Commentary,* ed. Frank E. Gaebelein (Grand Rapids, MI: Zondervan Publishing House, 1976), 10:155.

4. Ibid., 156.

Lesson 14/Greeting the Family of God
(16:1–27)

"I did it my way. I didn't have any help from anyone. I was totally on my own. I did a great job by myself. My success is just that—mine alone. It belongs to no one else but me."

Does that sound egotistical? You're right, it is. Does it sound selfish? Right again. But worse than that, it's simply not true—not for anyone. There isn't a human being—never has been and never will be—who hasn't drawn on someone's help at some time to do something. We come into this world with help, and we get through this world with help. We are dependent people, like it or not, acknowledge it or not.

The apostle Paul knew this. And to his credit, he not only accepted it but reveled in it. He loved the people he depended on. They were family to him, loved ones with incredible value because of who they were and what they did. He believed they deserved honor and respect, especially from fellow brothers and sisters in the faith. Christians, of all people, should embrace and support one another as family. Paul did that himself, and he expected other believers to do the same.

In the closing chapter of Romans, Paul spends the bulk of the space greeting various members of God's family in Rome (16:3–15) and offering greetings to all the Roman Christians on behalf of the believers who were with him, helping him with ministry (vv. 21–23). As we work through these closing verses, may we remember all those who have helped us along the way and renew our appreciation for them.

A DETAILS OVERVIEW

Some people remember names but not faces, while others have faces etched in their minds but can't recall names to save their lives. It appears that Paul, however, remembered a lot of names and faces. People he had met, worked with, helped, and been befriended by were people he would never forget, no matter how far away they were. So let's get to know some of these people through Paul's eyes.

In the chart below, list the individuals or families or groups Paul cites, the descriptive titles given them (such as, *countrymen* or *chosen in the Lord*), and the words used to welcome them (for instance, *greet* or *commend*).

PAUL'S FAMILY CIRCLE

NAMES	TITLES	WORDS OF WELCOME

How many people does Paul name in this chapter?

Why is it significant to mention someone by name?

 ## FAITH ALIVE

Who are some of the significant people in your life? You know, the ones who have really impacted you for good, the ones who have shaped you, been models of faith, manhood, or womanhood to you, run interference for you, stood by you regardless, or reproved you when no one else had the courage to. Some of them may have already passed on; others may have moved away; several may still be at your side. List them here; then, in the coming days, decide how you would like to thank them for what they have done for you. Then follow through with love and deep gratitude. You may surprise some of them, and you will assuredly make them feel honored and appreciated.

MY FAMILY OF FAITHFUL ONES

THEIR NAMES	MY GIFTS OF THANKS

Referring back to Paul's 'family' chart, what would you say made a real impression on Paul? People's station in life? How much money they had? What kind of clothes they wore? Who they networked with? What they did for a living? What?

FAITH ALIVE

What impresses you about others? Another way to ask this is, How do you size up people? What's your criteria? That will tell you a lot about what you deem important.

How does your list compare with Paul's? Do you see any places where you may have misplaced standards? What should you change them to? In other words, what would be some better biblical standards for deciding what really counts and what doesn't when it comes to people?

PAUL'S HALL OF APPRECIATION

Now that we've gained an overview, let's delve into more of the specifics, beginning with verses 1–16, then skipping to verses 21–24. (We'll go back and pick up verses 17–20 and 25–27 later.)

BEHIND THE SCENES

Since Paul admits that he had never been to Rome and yet he seems to know so many people there, we may reasonably ask how he ever got to know these folks. Bible commentator John Witmer provides a good explanation. He writes that the capital city of Rome attracted people from all across the empire. Although Paul himself had not been to Rome, he had been in many other large population cities, such as Jerusalem, Corinth, Philippi, Athens, and Ephesus, and so would have become acquainted with many travelers from Roman society. Witner notes Paul's obvious concern for people as exhibited by the fact that he kept up with where his friends were."[1]

As are all the people named in Romans 16, Phoebe is a Christian. What does Paul say about her that reveals this? (vv. 1, 2)

Why does he commend her to the Christians in Rome? (vv. 1, 2)

 ## WORD WEALTH

Phoebe (v. 1): Her name means "pure or radiant as the moon." She served the church in Cenchrea, a port city just a few miles east of Corinth. She probably carried the letter of Romans to the church in Rome, which would explain why Paul "commends" her to the Roman Christians.

Servant (v. 1): "This word may be translated 'servant' or 'minister' (as in Mark 9:35; John 2:5, 9; Rom. 13:4; 15:8), or 'deacon' (as in Phil. 1:1; 1 Tim. 3:8, 12), [suggesting] that Phoebe held a formally recognized office in the church at Cenchrea. [Some oppose this, feeling] that the requirements in 1 Tim. 3:12 [would render] it unlikely that Phoebe [or any woman] would be in the office of deacon. There [is] not . . . a consistent NT disposition against women in leading ministry roles."[2]

Helper (v. 2): This word could mean that Phoebe not only supported but funded worthy causes.[3]

Along with Phoebe, Paul gives extensive words of commendation to Priscilla and Aquila, a wife-and-husband team

(vv. 3–5). What did they do for him? To answer this, see also Acts 18:1–3, 18, 19, 24–28; 19:1.

BEHIND THE SCENES

Although the New Testament never explicitly says when and how Priscilla and Aquila risked their lives for Paul, the occasion may very well have been when Paul was in Ephesus and a riot broke out in reaction to his ministry (Acts 19). His life was certainly in danger there (1 Cor. 16:8, 9; 2 Cor. 1:8–10), and we know from other passages that this wife-husband team was with Paul just before this incident (1 Cor. 16:8, 19).

Phoebe and Priscilla are not the only women mentioned in Romans 16. Among the others Paul names are Mary (v. 6), Tryphena and Tryphosa (v. 12), Persis (v. 12), Rufus's mother (v. 13), and Nereus's sister (v. 15). Junia (v. 7) and Julia (v. 15) may also be women. The mere fact that he mentions so many women is incredible because of the very low social standing women had in the first-century Roman world. But notice, too, what he says about them. What does that tell you, not only about Paul's attitude toward and appreciation of women, but God's as well?

BEHIND THE SCENES

Did you notice that after Paul mentions Rufus's mother, he adds that she is his mother, too (v. 13)? Paul doesn't mean that she is his biological mother but that he experienced her motherly care. Philippians 3:8 makes it quite clear that Paul suffered great loss as a result of his acceptance of and dedication to Christ. If one loss Paul experienced was that of his own family's cutting him off because of his Christian conversion, perhaps Rufus's mother perceived his loneliness and hurt and reached out to comfort him. Whatever the occasion for her ministry to Paul, he was obviously very grateful for her service.

WORD WEALTH

Holy kiss (v. 16): A greeting meant to convey spiritual intimacy and affection between Christians. It usually involved a kiss on the cheek or forehead.

What would you say is the social parallel in our culture for the first-century's holy-kiss greeting?

Jumping to verses 21–24, we find eight more people singled out by Paul for honorable mention. We know the most about Timothy (v. 21), who was converted and discipled under Paul's ministry (Acts 16:1–3). Paul also penned two letters to Timothy, both of which have been preserved in the New Testament as 1 and 2 Timothy.

BIBLE EXTRA

To learn more about Timothy and his relationship to Paul, read 1 and 2 Timothy. They are short but packed letters, very practical and ministry-oriented.

Regarding Lucius, Jason, and Sosipater, we know next to nothing (Rom. 16:21). Lucius could be the Lucius mentioned in Acts 13:1, Jason might be the person who entertained Paul and his two assistants at Thessalonica (Acts 17:5), and Sosipater may be the Sopater named in Acts 20:4, but none of these identifications is certain. All we really know about these three men is that they were part of Paul's team in Corinth.

Tertius acted as Paul's secretary, actually penning Romans while Paul dictated it (Rom. 16:22).

Gaius extended his hospitality to Paul and the young Corinthian church (v. 23). There's a strong inclination to identify this Gaius with Titius Justus, the man who helped to establish the church in Corinth (Acts 18:7–11). If they are the same person, then his full name would be Gaius Titius Justus, which would fit with the custom among Romans of having three names.[4]

How does Paul describe Erastus? (Rom. 16:23)

 BEHIND THE SCENES

Archaeological excavations have provided a strong link between this Erastus and a civic official of the same name. An Erastus who was the Commissioner of Public Works in first-century Corinth paid for a stretch of pavement and got his name inscribed on one of the paving blocks. If this Erastus is the same one named by Paul in Romans, then by the time the ink was drying on Romans, Erastus had become the treasurer of Corinth.[5]

The last person Paul names, Quartus, may have been Tertius's blood brother. *Quartus* means "fourth" and *Tertius* means "third." Perhaps they had these names because Tertius was born third and Quartus fourth. These names may also indicate that these men were slaves. In the Roman Empire, slaves were given numbers for identification. Perhaps these believers were on loan to Paul by their owner.[6]

PEOPLE TO AVOID

After taking up so much space to praise and honor so many people, it seems ironic that Paul would spend four verses counseling the Roman believers to stay away from certain people, but that's just what he does (Rom. 16:17–20). Who are the people to keep at arm's length? What traits mark them for easy identification?

In your opinion, are these divisive people Christians or non-Christians or could they be either? Why do you think this?

What does it mean "to be wise in what is good, and simple concerning evil"? (v. 19)

Why do you think Paul mentions Satan in verse 20 and contrasts this fallen angel's activities with God's peace?

 FAITH ALIVE

How might you apply these four verses to your own life situation right now? Especially concentrate on how you can be wise in the good and simple in the evil.

A DOXOLOGY TO LIVE FOREVER BY

Paul closes his Magna Charta of the Christian gospel with a fitting benediction—a doxology designed to review once more how much God has done and is doing for us and how faithful He is to His promises (vv. 25–27).

What does Paul say about God in these verses?

About the gospel he preaches?

About Jesus Christ?

If you had been Paul writing the conclusion to this incredible letter, what would you have written? Draw upon what has meant the most to you in this study and put it in the form of praise to God and encouragement to other believers, as Paul did. Let these words stand as your summary of and refreshment in the gospel of Jesus Christ, our Lord and Savior forever. Amen.

1. John A. Witmer, "Romans," in *The Bible Knowledge Commentary: New Testament Edition,* eds. John F. Walvoord and Roy B. Zuck (Wheaton, IL: Victor Books, 1983), 498–499.

2. *Spirit-Filled Life Bible* (Nashville, TN: Thomas Nelson Publishers, 1991), 1714, note on 16:1.

3. Ibid., note on 16:2.

4. Everett F. Harrison, "Romans," in *The Expositor's Bible Commentary,* ed. Frank E. Gaebelein (Grand Rapids, MI: Zondervan Publishing House, 1976), 10:169.

5. F. F. Bruce, *The Epistle of Paul to the Romans,* Tyndale New Testament Commentaries, gen. ed. R. V. G. Tasker (Grand Rapids, MI: William B. Eerdmans Publishing Company, 1963), 280.

6. Ibid., 281.